D0432789

Interpreting Your

Dreams

Discover the Meaning of Your Dreams

This is a **FLAME TREE** book
First published in 2010

Publisher and Creative Director: Nick Wells
Project Editor: Catherine Taylor
Art Director: Mike Spender
Layout Design: Dave Jones
Digital Design and Production: Chris Herbert
Editorial and Picture Research: Sonya Newland

11 13 14 12 10
1 3 5 7 9 10 8 6 4 2

This edition first published 2010 by
FLAME TREE PUBLISHING
Crabtree Hall, Crabtree Lane
Fulham, London SW6 6TY
United Kingdom

www.flametreepublishing.com

Flame Tree Publishing is part of The Foundry Creative Media Co. Ltd
© 2010 This edition The Foundry Creative Media Company

ISBN 978-1-84786-705-6

A CIP record for this book is available from the British Library upon request.

All rights reserved. No part of this publication may be reproduced, stored in a retrieval system,
or transmitted in any form or by any means, electronic, mechanical, photocopying,
recording or otherwise, without the prior permission in writing of the publisher.

Printed in China

All pictures are courtesy of Shutterstock and © the following photographers:
1 & 63 Sean Prior; 3 & 10 & 52 Serg Zastavkin; 4 & 27 Colette3; 5b & 101 Melissa King; 5t & 83 Ingvald Kaldhussater; 6b AdamEdwards; 6t & 128 forestpath;
7b & 194 Photosani; 7t & 165 Chris Jenner ; 81, 200 ChipPix; 8b & 212 Shukaylov Roman; 8t & 210 Sandra Kemppainen ; 95, 144 Tom Mc Nemar; 9b & 126
Peter Doomen; 9t & 240 Phant; 11 & 43 Fiona Ayerst; 12 & 132 Artsiom Kireyau; 14 Nick Biemans; 17 BogdanBoev; 18 mlorenz; 20 Tischenko Irina;
21 Artizani Reclame; 23 Heiko Kiera; 24 Iarus; 25 Viaceslav K.; 29 worldswildlifewonders; 30 clickit ; 32 Naturablichter; 34 Lightpoet; 36 Lee Torrens; 38 Eduard
Kyslynskyy; 39 nikolpetr; 41 Gabi Siebenha; 45 Steve Herrmann; 46 istvanffy; 49 Valentyn Volkov; 50 dean bertoncelj; 54 tonobalaguerf; 56 Netfalls;
58 Poulsons Photography; 61 Reha Mark ; 64 ArrowStudio, LLC; 65 Piotr Marcinski; 67 ason; 69 Ronald Sumners; 71 Zurijeta; 73 Lynne Carpenter; 74 Yanick
Vallée; 77 Cio; 78 Torsten Schon; 80 Andrejs Pidjass; 84 Ewa Walicka; 87 denisk ; 88 MikeE; 91 picamaniac; 92 Marc Dietrich; 96 Christopher Futcher;
98 Phase4Photography; 102 Ivan Cholakov Gostock-dot-net; 105 Sibrikov Valery; 107 akva; 108 Kenneth V. Pilon; 110 Dirk Ercken; 112 Knud Nielsen; 115
Joe Gough; 116 kldy ; 119 Rohit Seth; 120 Dudarev Mikhail; 122 Rafa Irusta; 125 WilleeCole; 131 vesna cvorovic; 134 TheClarkester; 137 Feverpitch; 139
Loskutnikov; 141, 148 Fedor Selivanov; 142 filmfoto; 147 Patricia Hofmeester; 149 photobank.ch; 151 Roman Sigaev; 152 Simon Bratt; 154 Neil Roy Johnson;
157 jan kranendonk; 159 Ristoviita; 161 malamus; 162 jörg röse-oberreich; 167 Catmando; 168 chen; 170 Andrei Nekrassov; 172 nikkytok; 175 Inga Nielsen ;
177 Robyn Mackenzie; 178 Lena Lir; 180 Botond Horváth; 183 svefnlaus; 185 RazoomGame; 187 Svemir; 189 8781118005; 192 pirita; 197 maga; 198 Maria
Dryfhout; 202 Jozef Sedmak; 205 Mikhail Levit; 207 Scott Rothstein; 208 Timur Kulgarin; 215 Linda Brotkorb; 217 Konstantin Yolshin; 218 Neale Cousland;
221 Anton Balazh; 222 tatif55; 225 alehnia; 226 Lorraine Kourafas; 228 Ron Zmiri; 230 Mirenska Olga; 233 Fotokostic; 235 Matsonashvili Mikhail; 236 Richard
Griffin; 239 Radka Tesarova; 241 Nayashkova Olga; 243 Dusan Zidar; 244 Evgeny Karandaev; 247 Ramzi Hachicho; 248 ilker canikligil; 251 szefei.

Interpreting Your Dreams

Discover the Meaning of Your Dreams

WARRINGTON BOROUGH COUNCIL	
34143100379351	
Bertrams	15/06/2010
AN	£8.99
BIR	

ADAM FRONTERAS

General Editor: RASHID AHMAD

FLAME TREE
PUBLISHING

Contents

If we dream of animals they may still in fact represent people we know. Their animal form may simply be your mind's way of revealing the character and personality of somebody, or how you see them, via much more striking metaphorical means and without any preconceptions. Animals also embody various situations, prospects, emotions and feelings. This chapter reveals these and many more meanings of dreams containing animals and animal motifs of all sorts.

In this section, discover the meaning of everything from the different elements of anatomy, bodily functions, features, conditions and medical treatments to all sorts of articles of clothing, accessories, fabric, jewellery and clothes-making items. You will learn that to dream of kidneys warns of health problems, but that to dream of disease usually signifies good news, while a shirt can mean different things depending on its cleanliness.

Birth and death are two of the most basic and thus most important aspects of life. It is not surprising therefore that these events crop up frequently in dreams. Many motifs connected to childbirth and babies are covered in this section – from abortion to breastfeeding. Many more aspects related to violence, war and death are also covered – from weapons such as guns and swords, to the funereal motifs of pallbearer and hearse.

This section covers some of the 'classic' fears or negative situations that people dream about, such as failure, falling, isolation and humiliation – the latter, for example, can warn of arrogance in your behaviour. The section also discusses various motifs connected to crime and the law – from arrest to jail, both classic symbols of obstacles that need to be overcome.

Home can be the building or the area in which we live, the people with whom we live or where we come from. If we dream of home it may indicate satisfaction. We can also dream of rent and mortgages, which in fact symbolize mortgages and financial pressure respectively. This section covers all this and more.

Journey 154

Journeys in dreams do not necessarily reflect a journey in real life as much as they might suggest change, and travel-related motifs all carry their own significance. This section covers the meaning of general travel and voyage, before going on to explore more specific elements such as compass, road, destinations and the various means of transportation involved.

Work and Leisure 168

The day-to-day affairs of life are probably the most common feature of our dreams. We absorb so much information unconsciously during the day while at work, school or play, that our brains need to sift through this while we sleep in order to make sense of it and file it away. This section covers motifs from our everyday lives, from school to work to recreational pastimes.

Relationships

This section of the book begins with family – to dream of an uncle, for instance, can indicate an unpleasant bout of illness that will befall a family member. It then goes on to other people in general. Finally, love and marriage are explored, from kissing to divorce – which, depending on whether you are already married or not, can alternately indicate a doomed or stable relationship.

Beyond Earth

Sometimes our minds take us away from our day-to-day existence to explore places or situations we cannot experience in real life, or motifs and practices relating to the religious beliefs we or others hold. Of course, these all ultimately symbolize something relating to our own existence on this planet. This section discusses the meanings of magical, mysterious and out-of-this-world motifs.

Food and Environment 226

This section discusses the natural landscape, vegetation and plants, alongside the fundamentals of food, eating and drinking. All kinds of food are covered, from potatoes, carrots, strawberries and apples to walnuts, parsley, beef and lard. Weather and events outside of human control have powerful imagery – storms represent obstacles to be fought, while a rainbow makes your dreams come true.

Introduction

The external world functions in a state of rapid, perpetual flux and involves many interrelationships, which incorporate feelings and thoughts that originate from both yourself and other people; situations that may be ordinary or extraordinary, and all the subsequent information that arises from these relationships and situations.

Why Do We Dream?

The individual's journey through this cacophony is as varied and complex as it is important to the individual's development. It is not surprising, then, that in the midst of this confusion the human survival instinct surfaces and reinstates itself in the dream world, in an attempt to gain insight and understanding. The profusion and confusion of information operating in any given moment requires sifting and sorting out in order to give it form and sensibility.

Where Do Dreams Come From?

Firstly, there are the immediate sources: your home, family and friends. Add to these your own feelings and thoughts, in which you carry your hopes, fears and aspirations. This is your personal pool of information, that helps to shape your outlook and reactions to daily life. For example, an old house that you lived and played in as a child could be a comforting environment that you return to in your dreams, providing you with a sense of personal identity and security.

Then there is the body of information that comes from your social pool: people and situations that you encounter through work, business, education, dealings with the law and so on. Here you come into contact with the traditions, customs, ethics, values and principles by which society operates.

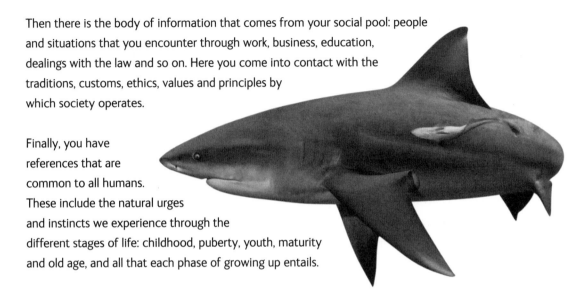

Finally, you have references that are common to all humans. These include the natural urges and instincts we experience through the different stages of life: childhood, puberty, youth, maturity and old age, and all that each phase of growing up entails.

The Dream Language

The dream world uses information collected by your senses from your waking life and reprocesses it, presenting it in a new way, so that you can understand yourself and others, and the nature of the details relevant to a situation, with a lot more clarity and truth.

The language of dreams codes itself in two ways:

 Literal: Presenting information directly parallel to everyday life.

 Symbolic: Representing the information in a coded form, disguised from everyday life.

The unconscious dream world uses signs, images, sensations and metaphors. The main form of information is presented in a visual way, although the unconscious will also use the other senses in order to draw the dreamer's attention to relevant details.

The main factor in understanding your dreams is crossing over the threshold of coding systems: from the logical conscious mind – which processes information in a sequential, linear order – to the more free-floating realm of the unconscious. In the unconscious, images and sensations float about as a minestrone of thoughts and feelings, which await selection and group together in order to give them coherence and meaning. These floating fragments of information remain non-associated or independent until enough components come together to form the basis of an answer to a question or puzzle, generated by the waking logical mind.

Keeping a Dream Journal

Here is a method for keeping your dream journal. Naturally, with practice, you may find a better and more effective method, but this is as good as any.

- **Keywords:** Whilst still dreaming, make mental notes using keywords. People are helping me/I am climbing alone, etc.

- **Remember:** Record the details straight into a Dictaphone, as soon as you wake up.

- **Feelings:** On waking, take a few minutes just to recall the salient feelings and write down on a notepad what you remember. This is very useful, particularly when there is a series or a recurring theme.

- **Interpret:** And finally, bear in mind that they are your personal dialogues and so the most qualified person to interpret your dreams is yourself.

What to Look For in Your Dreams

The theme: What was the general plot of the dream? Was it about a place, being chased, wearing clothes, a journey, drowning, falling, flying, snakes, and so on?

The action: What is happening? Where is it happening? (Is it a place you know from the past, or perhaps somewhere unknown to you?)

Your role: Were you central in the dream or were you peripheral to the action? This indicates your position and degree of significance in a situation in the real world.

The atmosphere/mood: Was it bright and clear, or dark and murky? Was it a scary or an enjoyable dream? Or perhaps it was about a competition. (Did you win the race?)

The environment: Was it on land, at sea, in the air or underground? By taking note of the terrain, we gain an insight into the root of the problem. Generally speaking, water represents emotions and land means money and self-worth, whilst air denotes the mind and thinking. To find yourself underground suggests reconnection with your true self.

Colours: Sometimes colour might be the significant feature of a dream and may be enough on its own to decipher the full meaning. On other occasions the colour might be incidental, but no less significant. Try to remember if one colour predominated.

Anagrams/numbers: These could hold valuable information about schedules, games of chance, significant dates and perhaps significant times when events will happen.

Characters, objects and animals: Different characters often symbolize facets of the dreamer's psyche or character, such as their masculine and feminine side, and will often surface in dreams if a particular part of the psyche is being repressed. They can also often act as metaphorical stand-ins and represent a situation that needs clarifying.

animals

Birds

All birds indicate the growth of our spiritual being in addition to the individual meanings of the birds themselves. They are said to relate to our wish for more spiritual heights in life and are therefore significant in relation to where we are going in life and in pointing the way to our higher life. Birds often bring with them a message: but one that you have to listen out for.

Aquatic Birds

Gull

An overseas messenger. If you dream of seagulls, be aware that you may receive unfortunate news from overseas. Also, this is a time when you need to be careful and not too trustful of persuasive, questionable schemes. If the gulls are flying over the sea, it indicates that you are unclear about your feelings regarding an issue overseas.

Albatross

A long-distance journey. While all birds indicate a quest for a higher spiritual level, dreaming of an albatross is said to indicate a wish to see the world, or the possibility of an overseas journey. Take heed of the sailors' warning: an albatross shot down indicates a stormy passage in your life.

Kingfisher

A sign of good fortune. Dreaming of a kingfisher indicates that success will be yours soon: the waiting has been worth it! With that success, prestige will follow and others will value you, and your efforts, much more. To see this iridescent fellow diving for fish means that you would benefit from taking a risk in a business proposition – but be precise and meticulous before diving into the depths.

Pelican

A spiritual message. Dreaming of pelicans is an indication of your ability to nurture others in a spiritual way. Pelicans in your dream indicate someone, normally yourself, who has an ability to get to the root of other people's problems – especially problems that lie deep in your subconscious.

Penguin

A message to relax. To dream of penguins may mean that you are behaving in an authoritarian manner with others. Although you may be acting with the best of intentions, others may feel that you are restricting them. To see penguins swimming suggests that you need to pay attention to the emotions of those around you. If you see Emperor penguins swimming, then leadership qualities will be conferred upon you soon.

Swan

A message of purity. To dream of swans symbolizes the purity of the vision and can indicate a celebration of marriage or engagement. However, be careful if the swan is singing, for it foretells an accident.

Birds of Prey

Wisdom, honour, regeneration... All these things may be inherent in a dream about different birds of prey.

Falcon

A symbol of honour. The falcon indicates that you will receive a message which will bring you prestige and honour; perhaps you will be honoured with an award or medal, or perhaps honoured publicly and gain an increase in your stature through recognition, possibly involving a promotion.

Eagle

A spiritual vision. Eagles, particularly in Native American mythology, have a very important spiritual meaning, which may hark back to the Aztec god, Quetzalcoatl, who was half-eagle, half-serpent. The eagle is a sign of spiritual vision and the rebirth of ideas. If you have dreamt of an eagle it indicates that you will achieve your goals. The higher the eagle is in the sky, the higher your prosperity and position.

Owl

A message from the wise. Owls are the companions of Athena, Goddess of Wisdom, and an owl in a dream indicates knowledge. It may also suggest a clairvoyant dream – of something that is going to happen in the future. Putting owl feathers under your pillow is said to help you develop the gift of foresight.

Vulture

End of a cycle and regeneration. A vulture, particularly one that is circling, indicates the end of a phase of life. The meaning of a dream involving vultures implies enemies and competitors are waiting for you to make a mistake, so complete whatever you are currently involved in and correct any mistakes as you go along. Soon a new era and lifestyle will dawn.

Songbirds

Blackbird

A dark omen. This can be quite an evil omen, as it is often indicative of magic used wrongly. The blackbird represents the shadow and it could be your shadow or someone else's. Blackbirds bring with them a message and it is important to listen to that message.

Crow

Time to turn ambitions into physical reality. To hear crows cawing indicates that you need to attend to your aspirations and begin to act upon them now. In dreams, a crow gives you magical insight and ability to see into future realities. Be warned, though, as a crow flying or circling represents being stuck in a situation through fear of future changes.

Magpie

A bird with a variety of messages. The magpie nursery rhyme has become so ingrained in our minds that its meaning is exactly the same in dreams: 'one for sorrow, two for joy, three for a girl, four for a boy', depending on the variation of the rhyme with which you were brought up. Magpies could also indicate an answer to a question that seems to be black and white but is not, so look again more closely between the lines and study the subtler colours that you find.

Pigeon

The ultimate messenger. Pigeons were traditionally used for carrying messages of importance. Dreaming of a pigeon means that you will receive a message at high speed – maybe even faster than email – as there may be some form of telepathic or clairvoyant link to this message. On receipt of this message, act upon it straight away.

Dove

A symbol of peace. In the Bible, a dove brought back an olive branch to Noah, and that symbol today is used as a sign of peace. Therefore, a dove in a dream represents peaceful times ahead. Also, white doves mean an end to quarrels – whilst a flock of doves suggests reunion with a very old friend, perhaps involving reconciliation.

Fowl

Chicken

A warning message. Dreaming of chickens is said to be a bad omen, as it brings trouble. In particular, the trouble is associated with partners, in both business and relationships, indicating that there is a need to tread carefully in these areas of your life. Traditionally, this dream meant that your partner was being unfaithful.

Turkey

A good harvest. The meaning of turkeys in dreams has changed over the years. Whereas it was once thought of as an ill omen, now, with its association with Christmas and Thanksgiving, it indicates a good harvest, the fruition of projects.

Cockerel

Dawn of a new event. Just as the cockerel greets each new dawn, the image in your dream signifies a new dawn in your life and suggests that it is time to start new projects. It is an uplifting dream that indicates a time of prosperity.

Duck

A message may be on its way. If you dream of seeing ducks in flight or walking towards you, a message is on its way to you by post or email. To see ducks swimming is good news regarding health, or if you have had health problems recently, then you will see an improvement.

Peacock

An omen for marriage. The peacock is an omen for meeting and possibly settling down with a beautiful man or woman. Business success is also prominent, particularly if the dream is around the time of opening a new enterprise. Peacocks in a dream can suggest a flowering of the libido energy. If the feathers were fanned out then they suggest you are seeking amorous attention, whereas if the feathers are down, they indicate modesty on display.

Reptiles, Amphibians and Insects

Seeing reptiles, amphibians or insects in dreams can mean anything from hints at wealth and prosperity to warning of an untrue friend. Snakes, in particular, are vital signs in dreams but, as with all animals, it is important to note the type, its actions and your own interaction with it to correctly interpret what the dream means.

Reptiles and Amphibians

Snake

Knowledge and temptation. In Ancient Egypt the snake was a symbol of rebirth (because it sheds its skin). A snake opened knowledge to man in the Garden of Eden; therefore, the snake also means knowledge. It also indicates the cycle of life, which is why a snake is used as a symbol in medicine. The nature and actions of the snake suggest different things in your dream:

 Sex: The snake is a strong phallic or sexual symbol and in a dream can represent the dreamer's libido, showing the repression of one's sexual feelings. This is particularly true if you dream that you have a snake coiled around you. To dream of being chased by a snake may mean that you are scared of the sexual advances of someone else. To be bitten by a snake indicates that you fear a sexual liaison. However, if someone else rescues you from the snake, then there is a longing for a relationship with that person.

 Letting go: Dreaming of your children playing with snakes can indicate a fear that they are growing up. This can mean you are overprotective of them, depending on their age.

Conquering fears: If you dream of handling snakes, then it means that you are conquering your fears. The type of snake you see will also be an indication of the type of fear you have. Generally, the bigger or more dangerous the snake is, the bigger the problem appears to you. A cobra, for instance, indicates that a situation is fast approaching and that you will have to manoeuvre quickly to resolve it. A grass snake, which is nonpoisonous, represents a smaller fear but much depends on whether it is pursuing you or not.

Past lives: An overriding fear of snakes in both sleep and waking life may indicate a hangover from a past life. Therefore, dreams of snakes bring with them a lot of emotional symbolism.

Emotional confusion: To see many snakes wriggling over each other represents many emotional issues intermingling and overlapping. It can also indicate a feeling of not handling relationships properly.

Commitment: To dream of a gorgon, such as Medusa with her head of snakes, indicates that you feel that you cannot commit to a relationship and, just as the gaze of Medusa was said to turn men to stone, the gaze is turning your heart to stone in this relationship.

Overcoming problems: To dream of walking over a pit of snakes, yet escaping without being hurt or killing the snakes, indicates that you will overcome any problems.

Pursuit: If you find that in your dream a snake approaches you and you chase it away, only for it to reappear in a later dream, it indicates that there is someone who is trying to pursue you. It suggests that possibly someone does not seem to want to take no for an answer.

Lizard

An insincere acquaintance. Lizards represent untrustworthy foes that you need to be on guard against. Lizards do have acute hearing, so the dispute could be caused by something that a friend heard.

Chameleon

Change with the circumstances. Just as a chameleon is able to blend into new surroundings and camouflage itself, this dream is a message suggesting that you will need to do the same. It is a warning that you may have to protect your true nature and blend into your surroundings.

Alligator

Caution required. An alligator in your dreams is a symbol of the mind's ability to move between the subconscious and conscious areas, represented by the water and the land. An alligator in a dream indicates caution regarding a new project and other people. The project or the people could affect your life dramatically, so be on your guard at all times, constantly weighing up your thoughts and feelings.

Crocodile

Caution required. If the crocodile does not move but just looks at you, it indicates that you have an untrustworthy friend. It is a message to stand your ground. If the crocodile chases or injures you, then you will lose out, but if you escaped, or killed the crocodile, then you will win through the efforts of your own tenacity and diligence.

Turtle or Tortoise

The turtle is slow but sure. Much that can be said about the tortoise is also true for the turtle, and both signify success if time is taken to achieve the results. Your dream may indicate that you have to slow down and avoid rushing a project, or you will lose it. There is a need to let things work at their own pace. The only difference between the tortoise and the turtle is that the turtle represents emotional projects with an aquatic link and may also suggest an event abroad, involving the nurturing of a young enterprise.

Frog

Frogs indicate success. Frogs are lucky in dreams as they represent luck in life and love. In a love situation, frogs can indicate a long and happy relationship. The frog lives on land and in water, which means that you are able to adapt easily to the situations around you.

Toad

Toads indicate success. Toads have a similar meaning to frogs in dreams. In a dream, it might be difficult to tell the two apart: if it is a toad that you see in your dream then you can expect success and luck in the future; this is good news financially. The toad could represent a trusted friend.

Winged Insects

Fly

Flies are enemies. If flies appear in your dream, as well as representing disease and infection, they can also mean that enemies are gathering around you. They are generally weak and jealous, but if you defeat them in your dreams, then you will defeat them in life.

Mosquito

Self-protection. To dream of mosquitoes is actually a good sign, as it means you are putting up a protective wall against others who are trying to harm you, enabling you to stand up to them.

Flea

To be irritated by the actions of others. To dream of fleas in the night indicates that you are annoyed by all the little problems that others are causing. If you see fleas on another person, then it can indicate that you are annoyed with that person and that they could be a problem for you. On the positive side, if you have pets, dreaming of fleas can also be your mind's internal warning system, telling you it is time to make sure your animals get treatment against fleas.

Moth

Family problems. In your dreams, if you find moth holes in clothes, it indicates family disappointment of some sort. If you see moths flying in your dreams, it can mean fighting within the family. To see moths flying towards a light source implies that others will gather around you, seeking your counsel and help in troubled times.

Butterfly or Caterpillar

A positive change. Generally, this is a good dream as you are going to hear from friends and people that you have not heard from in a while. However, there is a negative aspect to this dream, as these same people will leave your life just as quickly. It is also a dream of transformation and, just as the caterpillar changes into a butterfly, so your life may change soon, ushering in a new era.

Bee

Wealth and prosperity. To dream of bees is a sign that you are going to come into wealth and status, and honeybees in particular indicate wealth and prosperity. It is often used on a coat of arms and, therefore, dreaming of bees also represents prestige. Bees are also responsible for pollination and so they also represent fertility. For lovers to dream of eating honey indicates a wish for children. A vicar or priest dreaming of bees will see an increase in their congregation.

Wasp

Money disruptions. Wasps in a dream represent financial issues that need to be sorted out. For women in particular, it can often mean jealousy in other females who are envious of you, not just financially, but also socially. It is time to selectively remove ties that are retarding your progress.

Cricket

Listen to the inner voice. In Chinese mythology, the crickets' sound is one of cheering you along on a journey. However, it is also a sign to listen to your inner voice and trust your instincts to guide you, as your journey will be a hard one, fraught with pitfalls and surprises.

Wingless Insects and Creepy-crawlies

Bug

Sickness will follow. If you dream of bugs, then it is normally a message that illness is about to descend upon you – you are about to come down with a 'bug'.

Lice

Catching an illness. To dream that you are infected with lice can indicate that you are coming down with an illness. It is often found that dreaming of lice indicates that your body is developing an allergic skin reaction. Dreaming of lice on animals indicates hardship and financial problems.

Ant

Little worries make lots of work. To dream of ants indicates that you have lots of little problems; none of them is major in its own right, but together they are threatening to overwhelm you.

Spider

The web of life. It is thought that the spider's web represents the web of life and the spider is something that weaves the life of people. Therefore, spiders are generally thought of as lucky.

A climbing spider means success and a spider spinning a web means it could be spinning some money for you. The one exception is if you dream of a tarantula or a black widow spider: this means that a medical check-up is in order, particularly if it bit you.

Worm

Using worms as fish bait indicates a rapid increase in financial status. The bigger the worm in the dream, the bigger the objective and prize that you are out to catch. To see worms burrowing indicates that you are dealing with the unseen and need to use your intuition to create a path through to success.

Wild Animals

It is not unusual for large wild animals to suggest danger or to represent a warning sign of an impending struggle, but there is a multitude of other meanings. Horses indicate speed and beavers hard work, for example. The traits of the animal are usually a good pointer towards the reason for their presence in your dream.

Big Creatures

Bear

The bear indicates dealing with a friend. The meaning of the bear in your dream depends on whether the bear is aggressive or friendly. If the bear is chasing you in an aggressive manner, this means that a friend is trying to cause you a problem. If the bear appears friendly and you are able to stroke it, then a friend needs your help and support.

Elephant

A wise omen of the past. Elephants have always been associated with having long memories. An elephant is considered to be a wise and powerful omen and when it appears in a dream, it signifies something or someone coming from the past who will be able to help you on your way.

Giraffe

Look at the overall picture. The giraffe is known for its ability to see from a height and therefore in a dream is telling you to look at the overall project. Try to look at things from a detached, higher perspective and you will see the solution.

Rhinoceros

An aphrodisiac. Rhinoceroses' horns have always been thought to be a potent aphrodisiac and in dreams indicate your powers in sexual matters. However, if you see one chasing you, it means that you are scared of another person's sexual advances.

Hippopotamus

Perseverance and stamina. A dream featuring a hippopotamus indicates a need for perseverance. It can also be an indication that you feel unhappy with your own body and can be a warning to change your eating habits.

Monkey

Monkeys signify enemies. To dream of seeing monkeys indicates that you have enemies around, particularly in the workplace where monkeys represent working with incompetent people. If the monkeys are shown to be aggressive, then this would indicate underhand and malicious enemies at work.

Big Cats and Dogs

Lion

Pride comes before a fall. Lions are the king, of the jungle and in a dream can represent royalty. They are also a warning that you need to be protective of your family, but not to take pride too much as a virtue, otherwise problems will come your way.

Tiger

A struggle, but you win. The tiger has a strong mind and is powerful; it is able to take advantage of the opportunities that surround it. Effectively, you need to be like the tiger in your dreams and then you will succeed. If you are able to subdue or kill the tiger, then you will succeed. However, if the tiger is attacking you, then you will be the loser.

Leopard

Dangerous rivals: a leopard attacking you in a dream signifies opposition, so be careful where you place your confidences. To kill a leopard means that you will outwit your rivals.

Panther

A struggle or fight. Cats such as these are animals that are difficult to overcome; if you are able to track the animal down and kill it in your dream, then you will succeed in your venture.

Wolf

Beware of someone. Wolves have a strong association with the supernatural in our dreams. Wolves show a hidden side to our nature and they may reveal a hidden side to a friend. They have a tendency also to show financial influences. The nature of this dream will very much depend on whether you are the wolf, in which case you will be able to subdue the opposition, or if you are being chased by the wolf, whereby someone will be causing you financial problems and will be hiding the debt from you.

Fox

Foxes represent guile. 'Cunning' is a word we often associate with foxes and in dreams it means that you have to show the skills of the fox in your current situation. Vixens represent women with vixen-like traits.

Hyena

Someone is laughing at you. Just like the tradition of the laughing hyena, someone is laughing at your efforts and could be putting obstacles in your way. Be warned, someone is not as helpful as they may seem and you need to be wary. In some cultures, evil spirits were able to transform themselves into hyenas.

Small Mammals

Squirrel

Squirrels indicate saving for tomorrow. Just as a squirrel gathers a harvest of nuts to store for the winter months, this dream is warning you to prepare for what could be a lean time: a warning to save money rather than spend. If you are female, this dream can indicate that a shy person is seeking your attention.

Badger

The badger indicates good news. To dream of seeing a badger, which is in itself rare, means that you should receive news from someone that you have not seen or heard from in a long time. The tranquillity of the woodland setting indicates that the news will be good and will stir strong emotions. However, if you dream of an aggressive badger, this relates to pent-up anger over a friendship.

Mole

Moles indicate problems. To dream of being a mole, or of seeing a mole, means there may be problems ahead. The problems are probably hiding under the surface, but will soon break out unless they are resolved. Also, someone could be being deceitful to you and trying to weaken your financial foundation.

Ferret

Ferrets represent ideals. If you dream of ferrets, then it indicates that you would like to escape from the situation you are in. Perhaps you feel that you are destined for greater things in life. You will need to focus your mind on your work to find where you want to be in the future.

Otter

Otters symbolize curiosity. The otter indicates how helpful you are at sorting out other people's problems. Dreaming of an otter reveals your feminine and nurturing side, but also your ability to uncover the secrets that someone else is hiding, which they need help with.

Beaver

Indicates hard work. The beaver, of course, is known for building dams and working hard to protect itself from the elements. Like the beaver, this dream indicates the need to get down to work. Whether you need to start work on your own or with others will often depend on whether you have dreamt of seeing a couple of beavers working together or one by itself.

Mouse

Mice and rats represent our fears. If you dream of mice or rats, then this reveals your fears, and the likelihood is that they will get out of control. Prepare to confront and tackle the problems as soon as possible. Mice have very poor eyesight and it is just possible that you are not looking at your problems closely enough.

Bat

Bats mean that business dealings should be avoided. Bats in dreams generally indicate bad news; business deals should be avoided on the day that you have dreamt of them, particularly deals of a financial nature. The bat can represent someone who is deceitful and who is trying to close in on you. To see many bats indicates many people closing in on you.

Rabbit

Rabbits represent fertility; this sort of dream is often indicative of the prospect of children. Be prepared, as a dream of this nature may mean that a lot of expense is heading in your direction. You are certainly going to need plenty of energy to undertake new commitments. Pet rabbits in a dream indicate impending engagements and marriages. Hares, on the other hand, can be a sign of more general, unexpected, change to come.

Raccoon

Raccoons represent adaptation. Dreaming of a raccoon implies that you need to adapt to new circumstances; this may mean that you have to review your life and prepare to adapt to make the necessary changes in order to emerge into the future unscathed.

Porcupine

A need for protection. Whether you dream of a porcupine or a hedgehog, the meaning is the same: someone is trying to protect themselves; however, if you approach them carefully and with kindness they will open their heart to you. If you are dreaming that you are the porcupine, it indicates that you are trying to hide away from others.

Kangaroo

Thrift. Kangaroos hopping at speed indicate thrift and economical use of power. If you feel drawn to the joey in the pouch, then you are looking for the security that you had as a child. Kicking kangaroos indicate stiff rivalry and that you may need to prepare to defend your viewpoint against hostile critics.

Hoofed Mammals

Buffalo

A warning not to gorge. The buffalo was of great importance to the Native Americans; its appearance in their dreams signified that it was important to store up for what might be a harsh winter, although good times were near. The warning is to make sure that you save for the future.

Deer

Relationship issues. Deer in dreams can signify relationships. If the deer appear in their natural surroundings in your dream, all is going well for you. If the deer are in a zoo or an unusual environment, this dream acts as a warning that someone around you should not be trusted; their intentions are loaded with conditions.

Horse

Horses represent speed and power. We still use horses as a measurement of power in transport and in dreams they can signify the same thing. Therefore, to see a galloping horse is a sign of success. If you are fearful of the horse in your dream, it indicates that you are fearful of an experience in your life.

- **Status**: If you are riding the horse and are in control, status awaits. If, however, you are riding an uncontrolled horse, then your dream indicates that you are literally being taken for a ride: look at relationships and business issues very closely. If you dream that you are thrown from a horse, then it indicates a rival is going to cause problems for you.

- **Health**: If you are riding a horse that constantly bucks, it could indicate that you have a back or joint problem: this is your body's way of reminding you to pay attention to your health. If the horse kicks you, it is a warning that you should be aware of your actions and of those around you.

- **Success**: To dream of putting a bridle on a horse indicates that you are about to take on an unwanted task, but once you have completed the task you will be glad you made the effort. If you are able to shoe the animal, then success will come to you, even if it requires plenty of hard work. You will also find that your success turns out better than you planned.

- **Colour**: The colour of the horse is also significant in a dream: a white horse promotes the message and brings hope, whereas a black horse indicates delays. If you see black and white horses together, it is an indication that you need to ensure that you look at both sides of the issue. Colours in between black and white can lead to confusion. If you see Spanish or Arabic horses, this relates to romantic issues.

- **Friendship**: A stallion indicates success and someone with a powerful personality who will help you. If you dream that you are riding without a saddle or reins, and are amongst another group of horse riders, it indicates that you have many helpful friends.

Prosperity: To dream of a heavy horse pulling a plough indicates prosperity and rewards in financial endeavours. If, however, the horse is having difficulty, then you too will have to face obstacles.

Romance: If you are at the beginning of a relationship, then to dream of riding a horse uphill means that the romance will blossom and grow; on the other hand, if you are riding down a hill, then the relationship will follow suit and be downhill from now on.

Abuse: If you dream of using a whip on a horse, it indicates that you wish to dominate another person; it possibly also means that you wish to hurt them. This dream can act as a warning, as it may indicate that you are abusing someone else's trust in you.

Donkey

Attitude in relationships. The donkey in a dream tends to be closely related to any sexual relationship you may be having. If you are riding the donkey, or if the donkey seems peaceful, then there is no problem in the relationship. If it is refusing to move, then something is not quite right and one of you may be uncomfortable with the relationship. If the donkey is braying, then beware that a secret will be let out into the open.

Zebra

Take care and you will be rewarded. If you dream of the zebra, then take care (just as you would at a zebra crossing when crossing the road); as long as you are cautious in your ventures, they will be fruitful.

Camel

Endurance required. It is very positive to see a camel in your dream. However, just as the camel is able to go without food and water for days, you will also need to pace yourself. If you dream of camels coming towards you, which are laden with cloth and goods, expect some money or inheritance to come your way.

Domestic and Farm Animals

It is not unusual for our pets to appear in our dreams, but these usually have a different meaning to unknown but nonetheless domesticated animals or livestock. Their type may also have different meanings. For example, seeing a bull has a different significance to seeing a calf, so make sure you understand the nature of the animal in your dream.

Dogs and Cats

Dog

A man's best friend. Just like the saying, a dog in your dream can indicate a best friend, as dogs are loyal and do not question your judgement, sticking by you at all times. You do have to watch out for the tone of the dream, however; if the dog snarls or is otherwise unfriendly in the dream, a problem exists between you and a friend.

Cat

Beware another person. In dreams, cats represent ill luck and treachery unless you chase them away. Their appearance in dreams suggests that another person could be trying to steal your affections, while kittens indicate toying with affections in a playful manner.

Livestock

Bull

Competition awaits. To dream of a bull, particularly if you are male, indicates that a competitor is waiting in the wings for the affection of another. If you are female, it indicates a competitor for your affections. If you dream of a white bull, you will be successful in your relationship.

Cow

Abundance. Dreaming of cows generally brings good news and success in abundance. The only warning is if the cows are chasing you, or they are shown as lean and hungry, as that can indicate problems.

Calf

Successful plans. To dream of seeing a young calf indicates that you will be successful in any projects you are about to start. To see a calf carcass indicates disillusionment and even abandonment of potentially successful projects.

Sheep

A peaceful night's sleep. We count sheep to go to sleep and therefore sheep in a dream indicate a pleasant situation. To shear sheep means a successful and profitable enterprise will show rewards soon. To hold a fleece indicates a triumphant and successful conclusion to a personal ambition.

Goat

A warning about business involvements. If a goat appears in your dream, you need to be wary as the going could get tough. The goat represents the astrological sign of Capricorn, which refers to the goat as a symbol of ambition. If the goat is helping you in your dream, this is a positive sign. However, if the goat is behaving in an unruly manner, something or someone is hindering your progress in life.

Pig

Some cultures regard the pig as an unclean animal and therefore the persons represented are seen by yourself, or those around you, as being unclean and/or unsavoury in some way. To see a sow suckling indicates concerns and protective instincts, often relating to the nursing of children.

Aquatic Animals

From giant whales to tiny fish, dreaming of aquatic animals can suggest anything from fun to good fortune, depending on the type of creature. Dreaming of fish in particular can offer an insight into your own personality, hopes and fears.

In the Water

Fish

Fish represent our subconscious mind. Water, and in particular the sea, represents our subconscious mind, therefore fish have a very important influence in our dreams and indicate our feelings, particularly with regard to new projects. If the fish are swimming in clear, open water, then this is a strong indication of new prosperity. If the water is cloudy and polluted, then the project heralds emotional confusion. If you are fishing and you catch the fish, it means that you will have success in your current undertakings.

Like the fisherman who patiently waits to catch a fish, dreaming of fishing means that you may have to wait for success. However, your wait will be worth it. If you snare yourself on a fish hook in your dream, you are being warned against employing unscrupulous or deceptive tactics for the only person who will get ensnared in trouble is yourself.

If you dream frequently of being a fish, then it indicates that you prefer to use the subconscious part of your mind. You prefer to stay away from others; this dream suggests that you are trying to escape reality.

The species of fish that you see in your dream will have an influence on its meaning:

Eels: Represent a problem that needs to be looked at, otherwise your 'dreams' will slip away from you. They also relate to aspects of love and may indicate the slipping away of a partner.

Goldfish: Whether swimming in a pond or a bowl, goldfish are seen as a lucky omen in finances, while herring are the opposite. Salmon and trout indicate that your social life will be elevated, while sardines indicate involvement with social circles that will undermine your stature and position.

Tropical fish: Indicate ephemeral pleasures and that you can be scared of commitment.

Sharks: Denote other enemies: watch out, as they are after you. Be particularly careful with sharks; they represent a strong financial adversary. If you are having difficulties with finances and mortgages, etc., then it will not be a surprise dreaming of (loan) sharks pursuing you through the seas. If you see the fins from above the water in your dream, you should sort your finances out now, before the debts become too big to handle.

Seal

Seals represent balancing acts. Just as the seal balances a ball at the zoo, our mind uses the symbol of the seal to represent issues that we are trying to weigh up. If the seal is having trouble in your dream, it could be that you are trying to take on too much at this moment in time.

Dolphin or Porpoise

Dolphins or porpoises mean you have fun exploring your inner subconscious mind, suggesting that you should do this more often to awaken your psychic and imaginative gifts.

Whale

A large animal with a large meaning in dreams. Generally, a whale in a dream indicates the size of a project or problem in your life, implying that the issue on your mind is major and needs to be looked at thoroughly.

Shelled Animals

Crab

Sideways negotiations. Crabs indicate that you have got to side-step someone before they overtake you. You will have to employ some tricky tactics to ensure that you come out the winner in the negotiations.

Lobster

Repayment negotiations. If you see a lobster in your dream, it means that you will have to renegotiate loans. If you are eating the lobster, then these negotiations will be successful.

Mussel

Social negotiations. Mussels in a dream represent success in your social life and an increase in parties around the home. To eat clams is an omen denoting increasing social popularity.

Oyster

Sexual negotiations. Oysters are considered to be an aphrodisiac and are a sign of luck in affairs of the heart. This is especially true if, in your dream, you manage to prize open an oyster which reveals a pearl. If the oysters in your dream are off, then your partner does not deserve you. Oysters also imply that in business you may have to assert yourself more forcefully in order to reap the success of your hard work.

body and clothes

Anatomy

The way that you see your body in a dream can represent the way you see yourself in life. If you dream of what are considered to be negative aspects of one's body, such as body odour, it can indicate negative or self-deprecating feelings towards yourself.

Head and Facial Features

Head

Where the head is prominent in a dream, it is a message to focus the mind and bring your thoughts together: consideration must be given to what else is going on in the dream in order to discover which details are relevant.

If the head is floating without a body, it indicates that you need to use your head at the moment. Perhaps think before you act. If the head is larger than usual, then although there may be good news (in particular involving promotion) you need to be careful about being over-confident. If, on the other hand, your head is smaller than usual, then it indicates that you will achieve more than you think.

A pain in the head indicates that you should keep your secrets to yourself; however, if you dream that your head is on fire, then it can mean that you are being too aggressive or hot-headed.

If your or someone else's head appears to be on your body backwards, it demonstrates that you will need to look back over the past and resurrect an old passion, be it business or romance. If you do not recognize the head, this indicates that you are likely to meet an intellectual soon.

Forehead

If your dream consists of the image of your forehead, it indicates that you will achieve help from an unexpected source. If you dream of touching or kissing someone's forehead, then it indicates a very happy relationship. If your forehead in your dream is made of metal or stone, then you will have an enemy that you cannot make amends with. An injury to your forehead indicates a need to watch financial matters over the next few months.

Hair

Represents the spirit. Hair is important in dreams, as it is a good indicator of the way you are feeling. If the hair feels and looks good, it indicates that you feel good as well. If in your dream you are looking at the state of your own hair, it can mean that you are unhappy with it.

 Problems: Hair that is thinning or unhealthy in your dream indicates confidence problems. If you are for ever combing your hair, it indicates that there is an annoying problem; however, you will be able to sort it out but it will take time. If someone else is brushing your hair, then it indicates that you will need someone else's help to resolve the situation.

 Financial upheaval: If someone has tangles and dirty hair (including yourself), this indicates that the person is going to go through some pretty torrid times financially.

Friendships: To see a strange lady with beautiful hair suggests a new friendship is on the way and, if you are male, the possibility of a romantic opportunity. Long male hair in a dream is said to signify cowardice.

Relationships: If you are kissing someone's hair, then it means contentment in the relationship. A woman curling or colouring her hair indicates an improvement in relationships. If bleaching is involved, it indicates a relationship that you might be rushing into.

Success: If you dream that you are at the hairdresser's having your hair cut, then it indicates success in a new venture. If you are cutting someone else's hair, then it indicates a successful partnership. To have your hair plaited or have hair extensions added is good news, but not so good if it is someone else's hair, as this leads to arguments.

Identity crisis: To see yourself or someone else in a wig shows that you would like to change your identity and this dream often indicates a change of friendships and social groups; however, losing a wig indicates derision and people finding out things about you that you wish to remain a secret.

The colour of the hair is also important:

 Male hair turning black and curly indicates that you will be deceived.
 Going grey or seeing grey hair is an omen that someone in your family is ill.
 Red hair means unfaithfulness and changes.
 White hair indicates happiness and enjoyment.

Face

Faces in dreams have a message – if the face is smiling, then things are going to be good, but if grotesque, a business loss is possible. Looking in the mirror at your face denotes that you are not entirely happy with the way you have acted recently.

Facial Hair

A luxuriant beard on a man represents new business opportunities. On a woman, it brings unfortunate business dealings. A person wearing a grey beard, however, indicates that you will lose out in a quarrel with someone. To see a beard being shaven off suggests that you may lose out on a property deal. If a woman dreams of a beard on a man, it is a very good omen and indicates that she will meet someone soon: if he is young, she should be wary of his intentions.

Moustaches indicate that you must not let a small problem get the better of you. To shave off a moustache indicates a one-night-stand relationship that has not worked out.

Eyes

Look around you. Eyes in dreams mean that you may not be looking at things in the right way. The eyes also represent our soul. If you just see eyes in your dream and nothing else, it represents a change for the better. To get something stuck in your eye is a warning that someone is out to injure your business interests.

 Brown eyes mean a passionate affair but also that someone could deceive you.

 Blue eyes indicate a new friendship but they may also let you down.

Bushy eyebrows indicate surprise, while thin eyebrows mean that there is someone that you should be careful of trusting. A fear of going blind means that you are unwilling to change your mind over something, even though you know you should, but feel that you cannot give in. Long beautiful eyelashes mean a new and exciting love affair, but do not trust someone with no eyelashes, otherwise scandal is sure to follow.

Nose

To see your own nose in a dream means that you are feeling happy. To touch another person's nose or to have your nose touched indicates a romantic opportunity; however, a blocked nose points to financial problems, and dreaming of a cold nose may mean that you are preparing for a bout of flu or a cold.

Lips

Lips in dreams represent relationships and the fuller and sweeter-looking the lips, the better. If they are thin and cruel, it means that there are miserly tendencies.

Ear

Listen. If an ear plays a prominent part in a dream, it means that you are not listening to someone and this is likely to cause you problems. If you dream of many ears, then it can indicate that you are fearful of others overhearing you and finding out about your problems. Earache in a dream is a warning to get your ears checked out.

Teeth

Teeth in dreams are very common and are a very important indication of your emotional state. White and pristine teeth indicate that things are going well. Stained or tarnished teeth suggest difficulties building up through negligence. Teeth falling out indicate a phase of growth into new spheres of activities. If you dream that your teeth are knocked out by someone, this denotes financial problems brought about by that person. Other indications are:

- **Anger:** Clenched teeth in a dream are a sign of anger, and whether they are your teeth or another person's will determine the source of the anger: is it from you or towards you?

- **Unhappiness:** If you dream that your teeth are in an unhealthy state and going black, then it means that you feel unhappy with your relationship at the moment. The blacker the teeth, the worse the situation.

- **Legal problems:** If your teeth are suddenly longer than they should be, this points to a forthcoming legal issue.

- **Travel:** If someone has prominent or buck teeth, then travel opportunities are nearby.

- **Obstacles:** Brushing your teeth in a dream indicates that you will have obstacles to overcome. If the brush gets stuck in your dream, or you have to use a toothpick, this indicates an obstacle which still needs to be resolved. Picking your teeth for no other reason means that your friends will let you down.

Growing up: For a child, of course, dreaming that they are going to lose a milk tooth is an indication of the wish to grow up.

Dentistry

Dreams about teeth can also be a way for your subconscious to tell you it is time to visit the dentist. Going to the dentist is actually good news in a dream, as it represents sorting things out. Having teeth removed means that major transformations and upheavals in your life are about to take place. Having fillings points to help from another source, and gold teeth or crowns indicate financial help. Having root filling work indicates that you should dig deep into your resources and be more careful with financial speculations in the future. Having bridge work done to your teeth indicates that you have to pay more attention to your plans rather than hoping for the best. A set of false teeth signifies unexpected help from another person.

Teeth as Family and Friends

In dreams, it is also thought by some that teeth represent our family and best friends. The front teeth indicate children, brothers, sisters and other close relatives. The upper teeth represent males and the female family members are represented by the lower teeth. The eye or canine top teeth represent the father and the lower

canines the mother. Therefore, damage to a particular tooth could represent damage to the associated relative.

There is another school of thought, however, that suggests female teeth are on the left side and male teeth on the right, and that the whole mouth represents the house. Loss of teeth could also affect your finances, as each tooth lost represents a new family debt.

To dream of having animal teeth, such as those of a wolf or bat, means that you may need to take on the strength of that animal. Therefore, in your dream it will show you an area of your personality to focus on in order to succeed.

Other Anatomy

Neck
Financial opportunities. If the neck in your dream is broken, then fate will not be in your favour. If you dream that your neck grows in length, you will become more involved in other people's problems – bringing arguments when you offer your point of view in areas that do not concern you.

Back
Trust. If you dream of a bare back, whether it is yours or someone else's, it means you need to be aware of financial risks, as you could lose out, particularly if you are planning to lend someone money. Ill health should also be considered.

Arm
Good feelings. If you feel an injury in a particular area of your arm in your dream, then it may mean that you should get it checked out. Arms in dreams generally relate to friends and supportive colleagues, hence the phrase 'shoulder to shoulder'; however, if an arm should be chopped off in a dream, it means that a friendship will end through a lack of candour and trust in those around you.

Hands

Creativity. The meaning will be dictated more by what the hand is doing or touching than anything else. If your hands are doing things in a dream, it indicates that you will be using your skills in a work opportunity that will provide long-term rewards for you.

If the hands are grubby, then it indicates that you need to watch how you present yourself to others. Bent or old hands represent the easing of a financial burden, though you will have had to work hard for it. The left hand symbolizes romantic involvement that will fall apart due to deceit. The right hand denotes falling prey to the deception of others.

If your hands are covered in blood, then it suggests a family argument that needs to be resolved, and washing your hands means that you are able to take control of the situation. Otherwise, injured hands anticipate likely setbacks.

Fingers

Fingers indicate a direction. A finger pointing in a dream demonstrates where you are going, while a broken finger may indicate a need to retreat. If the finger is missing, then legal problems are likely to appear very soon. A cut finger means that you have done something wrong.

Long fingernails in dreams mean that you have a problem communicating with the opposite sex, though it will also show that you are endowed with scholarly attributes. Dreaming of damaged or chewed nails is a warning that perhaps a health check is in order.

Breast

Nurturing. For both males and females, a breast in a dream represents the need for emotional nurturing and comfort. It is a dream we face when we feel in need of support and indicates that we are feeling vulnerable. If you lay your head on someone's breast in your dream, it implies that the person you are lying on will be very supportive in the future. If you dream of yourself or someone else having more than two breasts or nipples, this suggests that you are being unfaithful. A dream where someone's nipples are pierced suggests that you want to win an argument with that person. If a woman dreams that her breasts are getting larger, this indicates the wish for a child.

Genitals

Sexual feelings. As one might suspect, dreaming of your genitals has a bearing on how you feel sexually at the moment and, as long as they look healthy and normal, then it does not represent a problem. If you dream of unhealthy or diseased genitals, then it could mean that you are being promiscuous: this is a warning of what could happen if you continue not taking the correct precautionary measures. If you dream of showing your genitals to others – in private or public – it may show an inclination towards exhibitionism. Pain in the genital area indicates the need to see a doctor.

Leg

Signifies decision-making. A leg in your dream indicates the ability to make a quick decision and move in a new direction. However, if there are problems with the legs in your dream, then it means that opportunities and decisions will be hampered. Skinny legs indicate embarrassment.

Foot

Journeys and obstacles through life. If you have an itch on your foot in your dream, then you are about to go on a journey. If your feet are just painful, then it means you have family problems. If you imagine your feet are on fire or burning, then someone is jealous of you and is out to cause you problems. Cold feet mean that you are having reservations about a relationship. Other aspects of feet in dreams include:

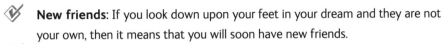

- **New friends**: If you look down upon your feet in your dream and they are not your own, then it means that you will soon have new friends.
- **Gossip**: If someone steps on your feet, then there is gossip around you.
- **Financial opportunities**: If you dream that your feet are covered in mud, then a financial opportunity will arise, but you need to be careful that others do not take advantage of you.
- **Financial loss**: If your foot was broken in your dream, then it would indicate that your financial loss was caused by your own carelessness. Seeing lots of feet in a dream means that finances really need to be sorted out quickly and the dream is letting you know that you should do something about it.
- **Humility**: If you kiss someone else's feet, then it indicates that you will have to gain a sense of humility in your dealings.
- **Scandal**: The worst dream to have of feet is when they are suddenly very swollen, as this implies a scandal is near. Divorce is also associated with swollen feet.
- **Warnings**: To dream that you have three or more feet implies that you may lose the use of one foot unless you are careful. It also means that you will be in charge of many people.
- **Happiness**: To see men and women dancing barefoot signifies friendships and happiness. If the music is not to your taste, then it would indicate that the friendships would be from a new circle of friends.

Internal Organs

Liver

A liver that is not functioning properly foretells that a quarrelsome, over-critical person who will enter your life, bringing disharmony and unnecessary problems. To eat liver in a dream indicates that a deceptive individual may come between you and your loved one. Prepare to root out the troublesome person who will gnaw at your patience.

Stomach

Trust. If you dream that you have a pain in this region at night, then, as long as there is no physical cause, this dream means that your health and strength will improve. However, if you dream of being bare-chested, this indicates unfaithfulness.

Bladder

Business problems. More often than not, dreaming of your bladder in the night is actually a signal that you need to go to the toilet. If this is not the case, then dreaming of a bladder indicates business problems and that you should be careful not to waste energies in fruitless tasks.

Kidneys

Take good care of yourself. To dream of your own kidneys means that you may require a health check; health problems could be due to overindulgence. Eating kidneys, however, is an indication of love affairs of a clandestine nature.

Bones

Bones represent structure. The saying 'the bare bones of the facts' indicates that this is a dream about stripping down problems to the basics. It is a time of looking at the structure of your life. Skeletons in a dream represent a need to sweep and start again. This can be a time of positive change and also often brings new friends and acquaintances. A skull, on the other hand, means that the changes will be swift and perhaps not as easy as you would have liked. In the end, though, the change will have been for the better. If you dream of pains in your bones, it would indicate a need to have a health check-up.

Muscles

Lack of social contacts. If you dream of showing off your muscles, it means that you need to widen your circle of friends. Painful muscles – providing you had not been overdoing it before you went to bed – indicate emotional difficulties. A woman dreaming of muscles means that extra effort is required over the next few months to get work done.

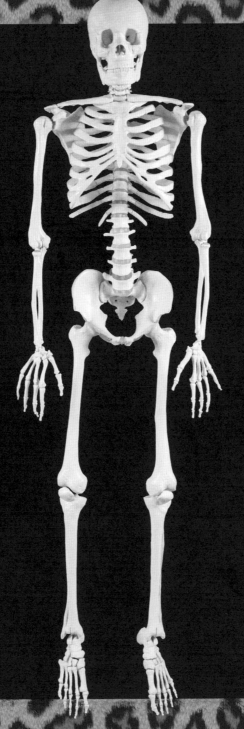

Body Aspects

From natural bodily functions such as urinating to issues of beauty and health, every detail in your dream may mean something. Whether these relate to yourself, members of your family, friends or strangers, note the detail of the body's behaviour.

Bodily Functions and Activity

Pulse

New activity. If you dream of taking your own pulse, it signifies that you will be starting a new and busy business prospect. However, if you dream that you are taking someone else's, it could mean that you lose out to their initiative.

Breathing

The life force. Breathing in a dream represents your own abilities and direction and, as long as it is pleasant, then there are no problems. However, if breathing is difficult, then it is a warning that your chest could be playing up. If you are a smoker, then it indicates that you want to give up.

Sleeping

Exhaustion. To dream that you are sleeping is an indication that you have been burning the candle at both ends. Psychologists think that dreaming of sleep is a wish to escape from reality, but one must also watch out for impending illness. If you dream of being asleep, it is a craving to be able to totally relax and indicates that family and personal problems have been heavy: your mind is effectively trying to work double time and put you into a deeper sleep. The dream will be modified by what you sleep on in your dream and naturally who with, and this may give further insight into your fears and hopes.

Crying

Good news. Crying in a dream indicates that things will get better; if a baby is crying, then good news is on its way. If the person crying in your dream is an adult, you will be called upon shortly to give help and advice.

Sex

Fantasy. Dreams of a sexual nature are very common and act as an emotional release and as a reassurance of your sexual identity and prowess. Sex with a stranger is a common fantasy and could represent a whim for sexual experience or experimentation. Alternatively, it indicates an identity crisis, where your personality is searching to consummate indiscriminately in order to understand itself better through absorbing the qualities of the person represented in the dream. Sex with your boss indicates a wish to be dominated, but also means that you admire your boss and therefore would like to possess the same leadership qualities. Sex with your partner in a dream acts as a reassurance of your love – strengthening and cementing the bond, especially if there have been bouts of low performance within your relationship.

Homosexuality

Insecurity. A dream of this nature is common regardless of your sexuality and indicates that you are thinking about sexual experimentation. If a heterosexual person dreams about homosexuality regularly, this reveals an underlying insecurity and non-communication with the opposite sex; it also indicates a strong desire to emulate and imbibe the qualities of the person you were entertaining in your dream. If you are homosexual, then this simply strengthens your erotic desires for the person you saw in your dream.

Body Odour

Self-esteem. The way that you see your body in a dream represents the way that you view yourself in life. Therefore, if you dream that you are perspiring or that you smell bad, it indicates that you have low self-esteem. If you see yourself or someone else sweating from hard work in your dream, it indicates that assertive action and positive self-image will require hard work but the rewards will be beneficial for all concerned.

Bathing

Renewal. Bathing in a dream symbolizes cleanliness and purification, and means that we are in need of relaxation. If the bath is empty, the dream is telling you not to make hasty decisions. If the temperature of the bath is not quite right, then this is a signal to adjust your plans. If you dream that you are shaving, whether in the bath or not, it means that you should not make important financial decisions for some months to come. Soaping yourself or another person in

the bath indicates that you should relax about a relationship that has started to develop; do not rush things and the relationship will begin to develop at its own pace.

Urine

Release of tension. Dreaming of urinating is quite often a signal that you need to visit the toilet. It is also, however, a sign that any tension that has been aggravating you is now released. This dream is telling you to concentrate on the future and not the past.

Excrement

Material gain. Although this dream is not the most pleasant one in the world, it does in fact represent material and commercial success. This is particularly true if a new venture is based on something from the past; you are now in a position to reap the rewards.

Vomit

Money issues. If you dream of being sick, then it usually relates to financial issues. If you are financially secure, this dream may mean that you will lose some money, whereas, if you are struggling financially you could find yourself a little better off.

Features and Health Problems

Beauty

New confidence. Dreaming of seeing beauty indicates that your heart is opening again and preparing for a new relationship; if you dream of someone dabbing perfume on beautiful skin, you will be happy. This is particularly true for women. The stronger the smell, the more passionate and fiery the relationship will be. If your nails suddenly grow longer or shine in your dream, you will receive news of a loved one from a distance. For a man to be aware of beauty in a dream reveals complicated business deals, brought about by a display of vanity that could upset things. For both sexes, the greater the joy at sensing beauty in the dream, the greater and deeper the passion will be in a new relationship, be it business or love.

Ugliness

Look into the heart. If you dream of seeing an ugly person, it means that help will come from an unexpected source. If you dream that you are ugly, it means that you are trying to project a false image and someone will see through you.

Injury

Hostility. If you dream of being injured, it indicates that others are showing unnecessary emotional hostility towards you; however, this situation is unlikely to involve any physical violence. If you dream of an injury to another person, then you need to examine your relationship with them to enable you to resolve the problems pleasantly.

Scalding

Minor obstacles. If you dream of scalding yourself, then it indicates minor obstacles; however, you will carry on and achieve your aims. To see someone else scalded indicates that you are going to help them through their obstacles.

Scars

Suffering. Dreaming of having scars on your body shows that you are having difficulties in life. The body part affected may indicate that you have very low self-esteem about that area. If you dream of scars on another person, it represents a period of instability and setbacks brought about by irritating arrangements that have been cast upon you unexpectedly from someone in need.

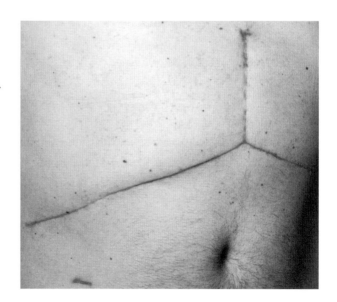

Mole

Omen. Moles are quite important in dreams; there are many psychics who read people's characters from the moles on their bodies: the larger and darker the mole, the more intense the meaning. The rounder the mole in your dream, the more good fortune should come your way. A mole on the right-hand side is luckier than a mole on the left. A hairy mole indicates bad luck. Dark moles mean quarrels that may be accompanied by a bout of illness.

Acne

Unhappiness. To dream of acne means that you are unhappy at the moment. In particular, this dream relates to your emotional life: you wish to unwrap yourself from a difficult relationship. If the acne is on yourself, it means that you are self-conscious about your appearance and self-image, particularly in respect of attracting the opposite sex.

Disease

Good health. Although it does depend on the type of disease, generally disease in dreams signifies good news, as it indicates that things will work out for you or the person with the disease. This dream may mean that you are going to fall ill, but if this is the case the illness tends to be mild. The exceptions are dreams about venereal diseases, which are a warning that your lifestyle needs to be considered.

Cough

Take care. To dream that you have a cough can of course indicate that you have a sore throat. Often it is a warning to take care of your home possessions. There is a need to check your house insurance is up to date, as you could lose something through fire, water, wind, damage or burglary.

Headache

Privacy. To dream of a headache means that you need to keep something private. Half of you feels that it would be a relief to tell someone but the other half is telling you that it would do more harm than good. You need to keep quiet about the issue at the moment.

Fever

Anxiety. To dream of a fever indicates that you are worrying too much: what you are worrying about may never happen. In fact, in all probability you are entering a very exciting period of your life, full of action and activity.

Pain

Embarrassment. If you are suffering from real pain in a dream you should consult a doctor to check that there is no physical cause. The meaning of the dream also depends on where the pain is. Generally, pain indicates embarrassment over the situation that you see in your dream.

Fatigue

Relax. If you feel fatigued in a dream it actually means that you will be able to relax a bit more in the coming weeks. Financial issues will dissipate a bit and you will find that you are able to recoup and enjoy life a little more.

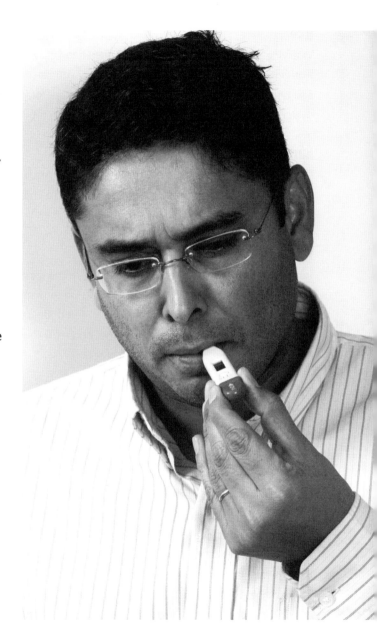

Itch

Worrying. If you dream you are itching, then it indicates a worry; however, there is no use worrying over this situation as there is nothing you can do about it until it is over. If someone else is itching in your dream, then it is an instruction for you to try to help that person overcome their fears.

Numbness

Change position. Numbness in a dream is often the result of lying awkwardly or being too constricted by bedclothes and therefore you need to change position. If you have this dream on a regular basis, it is advisable to have a check-up, as it could indicate nerve problems.

Paralysis

Inhibition. If you dream that you are in a state of paralysis, this can often be linked to sexual inhibition and emotional problems. You are going through a period where you want to fight against the current situation. There is a lack of confidence on your part and you may be unsure of yourself and your feelings towards other people. If this dream develops a regular pattern, it may be wise to seek some therapy of some sort.

Crippled

Help where required. If you dream that someone is crippled, then it indicates that you will be called upon to help someone out. If you are crippled in your dream, then you will receive the help that you need shortly.

Insanity

Realization. If you dream that you are going insane, it indicates that you are becoming more realistic about your direction. This dream reveals that you want to turn over a new leaf and go in a new direction in relation to work or a relationship. Often this dream means that you want to make life-changing decisions that will have a positive effect on you as a person but might seem insane to other people. If, however, someone else in your dream is going insane, then it is a warning to expect a sudden change of circumstances.

Obesity

Growth. If you dream that you are overweight, this means that good news is coming your way and that you are soon going to be in a position to financially indulge yourself. If you see other obese people in your dream, it means that ventures with that person will be profitable. If you suffer from an eating disorder, then this indicates that you view yourself as excessive in weight when in actual fact your body is simply being nourished and growing. If you are physically overweight and you dream of obesity, it indicates that your body is telling you to put on the stops and change your eating habits.

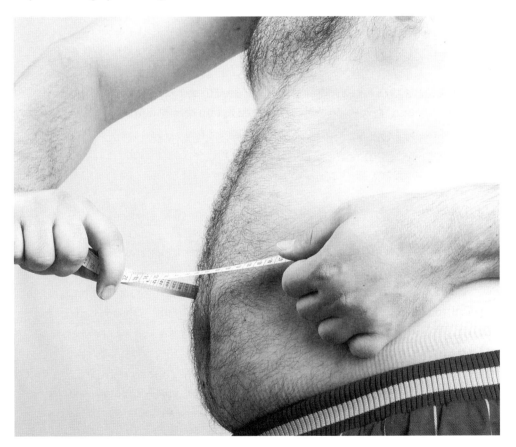

Mute

Do not do anything. The warning in this dream, if you see yourself or another person mute, is not to say anything or do anything in haste. It is time to hold back on your immediate thoughts and let things settle down. Hasty action could result in damaged relations for a long time to come.

Blindness

Deceit. If you or someone else is blind in your dream, then someone is being deceitful to the other. You are entering a decision without seeing the truth and this will cause a major problem for you if you are not careful.

Vertigo

Exploitation. Vertigo in a dream indicates that you need to be careful about a relationship in which you are being sexually exploited. You need to take control of the situation before you get hurt.

Treatment

Hospital

Overloaded. If you dream that you are being taken to hospital, it indicates that you cannot cope with the situations around you at the moment. You are perhaps very run down and tired and could do with some rest. There is a need to ensure that others take some of the pressure off you. If you visit someone in hospital in your dream, it means that someone is in need of your help.

Ambulance

An ambulance in a dream is essentially a warning to be careful, usually of sexual indiscretion rather than anything else. The flashing lights and warning sirens are telling you to hold back, as infidelity may be exciting but it may have repercussions for you.

Patient

Patience. Sometimes in dreams images are used instead of words, and sometimes the image represents something with a very similar spelling. This case is a classic example, where the image of a patient has nothing to do with health, but is a warning to be patient and take your time.

Doctor

Improvement. Generally, seeing a doctor in your dreams is good news, as it means that your health is improving. The part of you that the doctor is examining will lead to further clues in your dreams. The exception here is if the doctor is taking blood from you, which could be an indication that you are about to lose some money.

Nurse

Family matters. If you are a nurse, then this dream does not have the same significance. A single person dreaming that they are a nurse, or being nursed, indicates that they are going to meet someone that needs a lot of attention. If you are married or living with someone, then this dream can mean that you could be expecting a baby soon.

Psychiatrist

Advice. If you dream about yourself as a psychiatrist, it indicates that you feel that everyone is using you as a shoulder to cry on and that there is no one left for you to turn to. You want to find someone who is willing to listen to you for a change.

Surgery

Change in lifestyle. If you dream you are having surgery, or even performing surgery on someone else, then it indicates unexpected changes of lifestyle for you. The areas of the body will have significance that will enlighten you on the meaning of the dream. You can look up the name of the body part in this book to further understand your dream.

Amputation

Unexpected help. If you dream that you have a limb amputated, then it means that someone else will help you out of a situation. If your dream shows another person with one of their limbs amputated, then it indicates that you will help that person overcome their difficulty. The loss of a limb is more often associated with property rather than health.

Medicine

Unpleasant start. If you dream of taking medicine, then it means that you will have to do something you do not particularly want to do, but have to. Although the results might be unpleasant to start with, the circumstances will get better in the long run. Giving medicine to other people might also be a warning that you have to treat someone else with caution.

Clothing

In a dream, the more clothes you wear the more you will have to prepare financially. The fewer clothes you wear the easier things will be financially. The colour of the clothes also represents how you feel about the situations around you. If the colours are bright, whites, yellows and reds, you will be full of optimism. If all the colours are dark, deep shades, then it shows that you are aware of the responsibilities you face and have a strong knowledge.

Clothing Motifs

Wardrobe

Bank balance. Your wardrobe represents your bank balance in a dream and therefore an empty wardrobe means financial woes, though a full one will mean financial contentment. Finding a door in the back of the wardrobe indicates a wish to escape from your current situation and spend some of your bank balance on exotic excursions.

Laundry

Gossip. The saying that you do not wash your dirty laundry in public also applies to dreams. So if you dream that you are in a laundrette, it means that people will gossip about you. If you dream of washing your own laundry, it indicates that although there is hard work in your domestic life everything will come through in the end. If you dream that your laundry remains soiled even after having used the best soaps, prepare yourself for a rocky emotional spin involving a family argument that you will not be able to resolve quietly.

Uniform

Status. A man dreaming of a uniform can indicate a rise in status. For females, this type of dream traditionally meant that a new relationship opportunity would arise; however, nowadays

it also represents a promotional opportunity. Dreaming of a member of the opposite sex in a uniform could be a secret fantasy or wish.

Undressing

Secrets to hide. Avoid sharing secrets with new friends if you dream of someone of the opposite sex undressing, as they may take advantage of the knowledge they have of you, whereas someone of the same sex undressing will share a secret with you. If you see yourself undressing, it indicates that you would benefit by withdrawing from a relationship you are in. If the undressing is done in a provocative or erotic way in your dream, then it indicates a wish for sexual adventure.

Naked

Secrets out in the open. If you dream that you are naked in a non-sexual setting, it means that your secrets are out in the open. This is not necessarily bad news, as new opportunities will arise, providing you have nothing to hide. Seeing someone else naked is a warning of the same sort but that someone else's secrets will be revealed; however, you may not be prepared to hear them.

Being naked is about stripping away pretence and often shows your unconscious thoughts rather than thinking with the mind; it is the understanding of your emotional response to the situation that surrounds you. Other factors of the dream will give hints as to which areas need to be looked at. If you dream that you are swimming naked, this represents a need to understand your emotions. The clearer the water, then the clearer the solution will be.

Underclothes and Nightclothes

Corset

Confusion. If you dream of a corset, it indicates that you are confused at the moment, particularly over the way that someone has been following your every move. If you are having difficulty removing or putting on the corset, then this is an indication that there will be quarrels with friends that will make you feel as though you are too tightly bound.

Petticoat

Marital affairs. Changing petticoats could be an indication that you wish to change partners. Losing a petticoat means that someone else will steal your affection. The colour of the petticoat will also have an influence on the meaning: a red one will indicate a hot passionate affair, while a blue one means that you will meet someone who you feel is on the same spiritual or intellectual level as you.

Stockings

Changes. Putting on stockings generally means an upturn in business, whereas taking them off means that there will be changes in work for you. Getting ladders in your stockings means that you may find yourself in some short-term financial difficulty, but there will be a way out.

Pyjamas

This dream means that emotional issues need to be resolved. The dream is also common for couples going through problems and indicates that they may need to communicate with each other more when they have privacy, away from children and family.

Negligee

Relationships. If you are male and you dream of someone in a negligee, it represents a wish to be close to that person. If you are female and you see yourself wearing the negligee, it can mean that you want to be close to your partner but that you are having difficulty communicating with each other.

Tops

Shirt

New options. A clean shirt is a good omen indicating new opportunities, while a dirty shirt implies loss of a new opportunity. To lose your shirt in a dream is an indication that business is not going well and you need to take stock of the situation.

Coat

Financial opportunities. If the coat is new, then it represents new business opportunities; however, if the coat is the latest in fashion and is flamboyant, then your business is not going to succeed. Wearing someone else's coat indicates that you are going to ask that person for a financial loan. A torn coat indicates that your children will rebel against you.

Hood

Deception. To wear a hood indicates the need to hide. So if you are wearing a hood in your dream, then you are trying to hide from someone. If someone else is wearing a hood, then they are hiding from you. In all, this means that you are going to have to be more careful about who you trust.

Collar

Love affairs. There is the old saying that lipstick on the collar is the first thing a wife will look for if she feels her husband is having an affair. In dreams, a dirty collar indicates an affair. To put on a vicar's dog collar in your dream is a wish to do something more spiritual with your life.

Tie

Restriction. If you dream of ties, you are feeling restricted by your job or your personal circumstances at the moment. If the tie was loosened in your dream, it means that the restrictions will ease and you will feel that you are able to regain control of your life.

Dress

Putting on a new dress is indicative of an increase in social opportunities and may represent some upcoming parties. If the dress is very flamboyant, it means that you are looking for a romantic involvement; however, you should be careful as you may attract the wrong sort of Romeo.

Apron

Material gain. Seeing an apron is generally good news as it indicates your finances will improve. However, if the apron is torn, this can indicate family problems. If a female dreams of a torn apron, difficulties in educational pursuits will arise while, for a male, apron strings indicate a need to grow up and to become more independent.

Headwear

Hat

Your appearance to others. The interpretation of hats in dreams depends very much on what the dreamer is doing with the hat in the dream. Losing your hat in the wind indicates a recession is about to hit your business interests, while leaving your hat somewhere indicates a careless attitude to money. If you have a new hat, good luck will follow; however, if the hat in your dream is too small for you, this indicates conceit and overconfidence. A hat that is too large suggests that you feel unsure of your thoughts. A top hat signifies an increase in status.

Helmet

Problems. To see someone wearing a helmet in a dream indicates that someone else is hiding their true motives from you. If you are wearing the helmet in your dream, then you need to organize your plans properly and try not to be a scatterbrain. Often you are putting up a block and other people are unable to help you because you are hiding information from them.

Veil

Secrets. If you dream of a veil, then you are trying to keep something secret (and often in some sort of clandestine way) that you are scared of others finding out about. A funeral veil indicates disappointment and sorrow. A torn veil, whether on you or someone else, is interesting because it means that you will find out about a secret that will help you understand yourself better.

Glasses

Change of viewpoint. To see glasses on someone who does not need to wear them indicates that your relationship will change. If you do not wear glasses and you put a pair on in your dreams, then it indicates that you need to look around you, as you are oblivious to something important that is taking place in real life. Changing into dark glasses indicates that you will find a new interest that will illuminate an unseen talent that you have.

Footwear

Slippers

Domestic issues. If you are wearing a pair of slippers that seem comfortable, it indicates that you are very content at the moment. However, if someone other than your partner is looking at your slippers in your dream, then it indicates an affair.

Shoes

Opportunities. Shoes that are well polished indicate that there is going to be an opportunity at work. This is particularly true if you dream that you are buying them, as it represents the possibility of an interview. If the shoes are neat but well used, it shows that you should be wealthy in life. If you lose your shoes, it would indicate that you are wasting your efforts on something that is not going to work out.

Boots

Promotion. Boots that are well polished indicate that there will be promotion opportunities at work. This is particularly so if you dream that you are buying them, which represents an interview. However, if the boots are dirty, then there is a need to pay attention to yourself as you are creating the wrong impression with people. To dream that your boots are on someone else means that you have a rival in a love affair.

Heels

Sudden changes. If you dream that you break the heel of a shoe in your dream, then a long-term friendship will suddenly break up. Dreaming of repairing your own heels represents problems at a party. Dreaming of wearing platform heels indicates that you want to be noticed.

Accessories and Details

They say the devil is in the detail and, when it comes to dreams, nothing could be truer. Pay close attention to the details of dress – the accessories and adornments. They can sometimes reveal more than other items of clothing.

Accessories

Gloves

Security. Gloves in dreams are said to represent how we feel in regard to emotional and financial security. New gloves indicate financial security and, as you can imagine, losing gloves represents the loss of security. Finding a pair of gloves indicates that someone will help you with your current problems.

Belt

Financial issues. To dream of your belt is an indication that you need to watch your finances. Chances are that you will have to tighten your belt, as they say. To dream that you have a brand new belt indicates that you are about to enter into negotiations with the bank.

Buttons

Buttons represent money in dreams. To have bright new ones, particularly gold buttons, indicates that you are going to come into some money. Losing buttons means that you are going to have financial difficulties. Cloth-covered buttons denote sadness.

Knots

A reminder. A knot represents something that you should not forget to do. It also represents an obstacle and, as long as you succeed in untying the knot, you will succeed in resolving the problem. If you live by the coast or work at sea, then it is an indication of windy weather to come.

Decorations

Jewellery

Generally a good omen. Being given jewellery or giving it to someone else symbolizes love and affection. If you dream that you are stealing jewellery, then it means that you need to take very good care of your business at the moment. A tiara in a dream is indicative of a crown and therefore represents honour and a rise in status.

 Earrings: These are, of course, related to the ear and mean that you need to listen carefully to enable you to take advantage of the situations around you. However, this dream can mean that you need to be careful of repeating what you hear.

 Necklaces: Good for romance and love, providing it does not break or get damaged, which represents quarrels. If you dream that you are given a locket, this is good news for relationships, as it indicates a long commitment and marriage, plus lots of children.

Bracelets: Long-term friendships and relationships. It is a fortunate time for you as long as the bracelet is not broken, which indicates the loss of friendship. If you have just met a new partner and you have dreamt of a bracelet, this dream foretells that your engagement is in the near future.

 Rings: Commitment in long-term relationships. To give or be given a ring is of particular significance as this indicates a forthcoming marriage or engagement. If you lose a ring, then it does not necessarily mean the opposite, but instead can mean that you will have good news in business. Rings stand for the eternity of a relationship. To see two rings intertwined in a dream indicates the start of a very close and long-lasting relationship. To dream of broken rings is a signal of a broken relationship and broken hearts.

If you take jewellery from a jewellery box to try it on, this means that you feel you are stagnating and not getting out and about enough. To put the jewellery in the box indicates that you are happy being at home and want to be able to spend some quality time with your family.

Cufflinks

Opportunities to impress. If you are a man and you dream of wearing cufflinks, then it indicates a job opportunity for you, where you will have the chance to impress. If the cufflinks are decorated – the decoration may add more insight to your dream – you will do well in an interview and will have plenty of confidence.

Ribbons

Ribbons are connected to relationships. If you dream of new ribbons, then it means that there is a new partner on the way. It is worth noting the colour of the ribbon, as this will indicate what the basis of the relationship is. Red ribbons signify passionate love, while green ribbons signify jealousy. Yellow ribbons show an emergence of independent thinking. Blue indicates a soul-to-soul kinship forming and black is a sign to let go of the old ways and habits that may have sapped your energy in the past.

Bow

A reminder. A bow or bow tie is like a knot in a piece of string and in a dream represents something that you should not forget to do. A flamboyant bow tie in your dream means that you want to show off your individuality.

Fabric, Materials and Clothes-making

The type of material from which your dream clothing is made is extremely important, although if your clothing fabrics are transparent, this is a positive omen, perhaps suggesting prosperity or luxurious times ahead!

Fabric

Silk

Luxury. Although this dream is one that shows a forthcoming time of luxury, it also warns that you must not rest on your laurels. To dream that you or your partner are dressed in silk means that you feel happy when you are close to that person. If your dream is about old silk, then you may receive a present from an elderly relative.

Velvet

Luxury. Velvet in dreams represents opulence; the area of your life that it may affect will depend on the colour. Purple represents royalty or the Church. Red represents matters of the heart, blue is for commerce, green is for luck.

Leather

A positive omen. Leather is always considered a good omen in a dream and generally promises successful business and romantic liaisons. Ornaments made out of leather indicate a very strong marriage or commitment.

Furs

Prosperity. If you dream of dealing with or wearing furs, then you will do well financially. It is a warning, however, that you should not get involved in arguments at the moment as you may not win.

Wool

Opportunities. If you see wool in a dream, it means that you are going to experience new opportunities in a new job. However, if the wool is dirty, it means that you will not have much in common with your new colleagues.

Rubber

Lack of worries. Dreaming of rubber indicates that you have very little to worry about. In fact, dreaming of wearing rubber suggests that you are able to break free of restrictions. It does, however, indicate that you are quite secretive in your dealings with others.

Clothes-making

Tailor

Travel. To dream of seeing a tailor brings unexpected travel arrangements. If you talk to a tailor in your dream, there will be arguments in the future. If you saw a tailor measuring you up in your dream, much care and diplomacy is needed if you want to avoid giving your strength away to someone else.

Dye

Change. Just as we are able to change the appearance of a cloth by dyeing it, in our dreams it means that we are about to change the appearance of our life. Changing a cloth to bright colours indicates a change for the better. Dyeing it golden indicates a financial benefit and dyeing it black means sorrow.

Sewing

Preparation. If you dream someone is sewing, then this dream is telling you to prepare for the future, particularly in regard to long term issues, such as pensions and investments. Leaving sewing unfinished is a sign that you have not sorted things out properly. Mending things with thread shows that you are going to sort things out soon, particularly if you are near completion. However, if you dream of darning, then the chances are you have left it too late and you are going to have to work really hard to sort out your future retirement.

Knitting

Contentment. To dream of knitting is a sign that you are contented. Conversely, dropping a stitch or having to unravel indicates that there will be some domestic arguments.

Spinning

Perseverance. To dream that you are spinning wool indicates that you need to persevere, particularly at this time in your life. You are diligent and will get your rewards when the time comes. Take your time, however, and be very patient.

Weaving

Contentment if all goes well. If you are contentedly weaving in your dreams, then life is going to go smoothly. However, if you get knots or tangles when weaving in your dream, you will encounter problems that you will need to overcome.

Loom

One step back to move forward. To dream of a loom means that you will need to adjust your current situation, even if this means taking a change of direction. You are feeling irritated but everything will work out for you in the end. To see a loom in your dream with no one working it, however, implies that you are being too stubborn at the moment.

Thimble

Marriage. Regardless of your gender, dreaming of a thimble brings domestic contentment and a happy married life. If the thimble collection grows in your dream, so shall the contentment in your life. To lose a thimble, however, indicates marital strife.

Thread

Gossip. Finding loose thread on your or someone else's clothing indicates that you will be involved in idle gossip over the next few days. Long pieces of thread indicate that you are not taking the best path with regard to your work; a re-structure of your long-term goals and aspirations would help.

Needle

Ease or frustration. If you are threading a needle in your dream, then it indicates an obstacle. How well you thread the needle will dictate how well you cope with the obstacle. If you get angry with frustration or prick yourself, then you will find it difficult to cope with the situation.

Scissors

Prompt action required. Scissors in a dream are a warning that you must do something fast, normally in the next few days. There are often associations with a relationship and scissors will break a relationship apart. This is normally due to a rival in love and so to avoid the problem you have the chance of rectifying the situation quickly.

Gems and Precious Metals

Jewels in a dream represent truth and will very much depend on the type of stone and its colour. The shape of the jewel is also important and, broadly speaking, a round or heart shape will relate to romantic issues, whereas angular shapes seem to be more practical in nature. The wearing of jewels means that your status will increase in the eyes of others.

Gems

Diamond

A girl's best friend. Giving or receiving diamonds in a dream is a sign of commitment to a relationship and symbolizes your desire to settle down with the person you are with.

Pearl

Emotions. Although classed as a gem, pearl is not a stone. In a dream, pearls represent our emotions and in particular those towards our family, especially mothers and children; or they can mean that family concerns need to be put first. If your string of pearls breaks, it can mean problems within the family that need to be sorted out in a caring, motherly way.

Ruby

The heart. The ruby represents the heart and, in a dream, it brings love and optimism to the situation. This dream indicates that you are feeling very positive and full of energy and that you will be able to generate enthusiasm in others with your plans at the moment. Losing a ruby can indicate losing your love.

Amethyst

The mind. To see amethysts in your dreams means that you need to take your time over decisions that need to be made shortly. It is a warning not to allow yourself to be rushed into things you might later regret. Amethysts in dreams signify understanding your needs.

Sapphire

Clarity and protection. There are two types of sapphire that you might come across in a dream. The first one is a blue sapphire and it gives you the knowledge that you need to look clearly at a situation; otherwise, the answers you need will be clear in the next few weeks. The other type of sapphire is the star sapphire, which, as well as the above meaning, also gives great protection and help from higher authority figures.

Topaz

Personal power. Topaz in a dream brings with it the opportunities of leadership. This dream indicates that you need to take responsibility, not just for yourself but also others, by delegating and getting the others to help you. Losing topaz in a dream means that you are being autocratic in your dealings.

Turquoise

Be alert. To see turquoise is a warning that you need to be on your guard and to pay close attention to what is going on around you. As long as you remain alert, then you will be able to take advantage of the situation. If you do not, then someone will take advantage of you.

Emerald

To see emeralds in a dream indicates that you will come into property and is a sign of good fortune. Emeralds also indicate honesty in friendship and promote growth in all relationship matters. Investment in Asian-based industries and commercial enterprises should do well for you over the next few months.

Jade

Intuition. If you see the green stone jade in a dream, it means that you should trust your intuition. Look at your problems and trust your feelings, as your instincts will tell you the right way to proceed. Jade also represents our ancestors, so it may be that we are receiving helpful advice from departed relatives.

Precious Metals

Gold

Fame and fortune. Gold in dreams is very significant, but the meaning of your dream will depend very much on how you discover the gold. If you are trying to find gold either by panning in a river or stream, or by just looking around for it on the ground, this means that you can effect a beneficial change in your circumstances by taking action. If, however, you are trying to find gold by mining, this indicates that, although you will be successful with a financial venture, there could be a lot of family squabbling. Other interpretations include:

Fool's gold: If you dream that you find gold that turns out to be something different, then you may have found fool's gold. This means you should look in your heart, not just at your bank balance, to find the right direction in life.

Hidden gold: Losing gold in your dream represents the loss of money. However, hiding gold indicates that at the moment you are putting finances before anything else and this is causing problems in your relationship.

Gold nuggets: Gold in nuggets or coins represents financial rewards and prosperity. Gold in clothes such as golden-coloured embroidery often indicates a rise in status and authority.

Silver
Do not overvalue money. Although finding silver in your dream is generally a good sign for moderate financial improvements, there is also a warning that you could be depending too much on money. You are also warned against making rash and hasty decisions; you should also be putting spiritual ideas before financial matters.

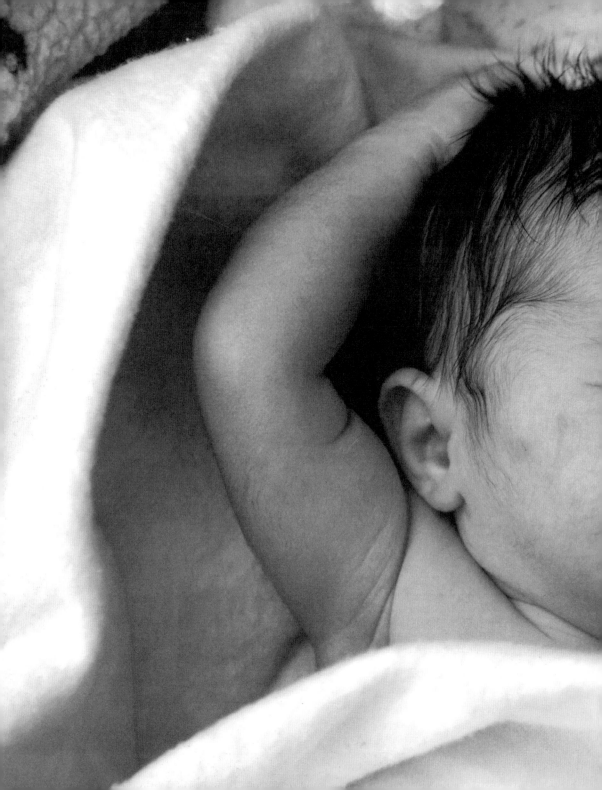

life and death

Pregnancy and Birth

In its most obvious symbolism, pregnancy in dreams can indicate that you are going to have a baby, and babies themselves can be a sign of contentment – but read on to discover the complexities.

Pregnancy

Pregnancy

Fertility. To dream of pregnancy may indicate that you are actually going to have a baby. Many women dream that they are pregnant and feel pregnant before any tests can prove one way or the other. However, it may be the body's way of telling the mind that changes need to be made. On the other hand, pregnancy in a dream can be a warning against infidelity.

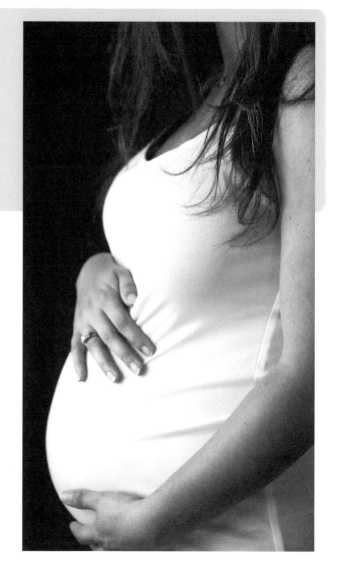

Abortion

Fear of failure. Very emotional dreams such as this have a different meaning depending which sex you are. If you are a woman and are pregnant or contemplating pregnancy, this is just an anxiety dream, although if you are healthy, it indicates that you need to check your health. For men, it means failure in a current relationship.

Miscarriage

Fear of failure. If you are pregnant and have dreamt of having a miscarriage, then you are suffering from pangs of anxiety, understandably concerning the birth of your child. If you are not pregnant, however, then this dream indicates fear of failure. It is common among people who have had this particular type of dream to feel that they have failed their parents in some way.

Birth

Midwife

Sickness and illness. To see a midwife in your dream means that you could be suffering from ill health. This may relate to the time when midwives were local wise women or witches who, with their knowledge of herbs, administered treatments for ailments.

Childbirth

Fertility. Childbirth often indicates that fertility is on your mind and could bring news about a forthcoming pregnancy. If you are not pregnant and are not planning to get pregnant, then this dream indicates accomplishments in work that you are about to undertake; they will be successful but a lot of hard work will be required.

Stillborn Child

Distress. To dream of a stillborn child if you are not pregnant indicates that you will receive some distressing news. If you are pregnant, this is just an anxiety dream and most probably everything is well; however, if you are worried about your pregnancy, you should consult your GP for advice.

Deformed Birth

Sort yourself out. If you have dreamt of a deformed birth, it indicates that all will be well in the future, but there are issues at home that need to be sorted out; someone is undermining your position and this needs to be sorted out.

Baby

Contentment. At its basic level, dreaming of babies is a sign of contentment and happiness in a relationship. It can indicate a wish to settle down and have children, particularly if you have dreamt of many babies. The baby's temperament also has an influence; for instance, if the baby is happy, you will have many friends. If you dream of a crying or ill baby, this can indicate disappointments that are to come and troubles ahead.

Twins

Double meanings. Dreaming of twins means that you have to be aware of the negative and positive aspects of the dream. If the twins are happy, then your work will be doubly rewarded. If they are shown as unhealthy, then you are in for double the trouble.

Breastfeeding

Nurturing. For both males and females, breastfeeding in a dream represents the need for emotional nurturing and comfort. It is a dream we face when we are in need of support and indicates that we are feeling vulnerable at the time.

Cot

Changes for the better. To dream of being in a cot signifies that events are going to change for the better. Many cots in your dream indicate that you will have friends around to support you. However, if you dream of a rocking cradle, it indicates that someone is gossiping about you.

Nanny

Trying to turn the clock back. If a nanny appears in your dream, it means that you wish you could change a situation from the past. You need to be cautious of arguments with relatives.

Birthday

Good luck. To dream of a birthday indicates celebrations and enjoyment. To receive presents or to give them indicates progress in your life. If you had difficulty blowing out the candles, it heralds poverty and false friends, with gossip or rumours about you circulating.

Violence and War

To see a battle in your dream represents an internal struggle. It can represent a battle that you are having with a friend or loved one and is a warning to sort things out before they get worse. Other forms of violence or related military imagery can be interpreted in different ways.

Battle Scenarios

Fight

A decision. A fight in a dream means you are struggling with a decision that needs to be made. The outcome in your dream will have a bearing on the success of this decision. To lose the fight means loss of home; to emerge triumphant implies that you will overcome the opposition and win any legal matters pending. To see fighting among others means that you have squandered money, leaving you with a bad business reputation.

Explosion

Improvements. Explosions in your dreams indicate that you are about to go through an explosive time, although changes for the better will be made. It is also a time to pay attention to business decisions that need to be made: make sure that you get the best possible deal.

Shooting

Disputes. Shooting someone in your dream indicates that you have a dispute with them. There is a need to curb your temper and to sit down and discuss the problems if you want to resolve them. If you do not resolve the problems, the situation could get worse. To be shot by someone else indicates that you will suffer at the hands of evil people and may suffer some illness.

Killing

A period of misfortune or stress. If you dream of killing someone, whether on purpose or by accident, then you need to curb your temper. This type of dream indicates that you may be facing a period of emotional stress. However, killing animals in dreams generally means good news will come your way: you will be successful, overcome obstacles and achieve all that you desire. To dream of killing someone also indicates that you are under a lot of emotional pressure at the moment.

Devastation

Control your temper. To dream of devastation and the ruin of others means that you need to curb your temper. If you do so, you will settle any arguments and all will be well. Otherwise, you could lose your friends and your liberty. To see the devastation of a building suggests that you urgently need to re-evaluate your skills and abilities, as your foundations may not be as solid as you believe they are.

Victory

Decisions have been reached. Battles of any type in dreams represent decisions that we have to make about current issues. To win a battle signifies solving a problem, but make sure that you listen to the point of view of the person that you are fighting with or you will leave yourself open to attack through lack of information about the issues. Winning a battle in dreams means that you have overcome the problem, whilst losing a battle indicates that you may need help from friends who can help you with decisions.

Armed Forces

Navy

Victory over obstacles. If the Navy appears in your dream, then it indicates that you will be able to overcome obstacles that are in your way. It can also mean a holiday is in store for you once things have settled down.

Cavalry

Rescue. Just like the old Western films, if you see the cavalry charging into your dream, it indicates that metaphorically a rescue party will arrive to save you from a problem that you are facing at the moment.

Fleet

Decision changes. To see a fleet of ships or aeroplanes indicates that you need to make some changes to your business plans. If you dream of a fleet of aeroplanes, then an immediate decision has to be made. This could also be an augury of pending war on the horizon in foreign countries.

Submarine

Deep emotional disputes. A submarine in your dream indicates that you are struggling with your emotions and that you need to resolve some relationship difficulties. If the submarine in your dream is following a steady direction, you will find it easier to resolve your relationship problems. The deeper the submarine dives, the more entrenched is the unspoken problem. So fathom the emotional depths of your history together with your partner and clarify the seeds of discontent.

Soldier

Reputation. For a woman to see soldiers (particularly in huge numbers) implies wanton romantic self-indulgence. For a man to dream that he is a good, noble soldier means that he will honour his principles and will reap the fulfilment of his ideals.

Colonel

Loss of position. To see a colonel in your dreams means that you will lose out in a job opportunity. If you were the colonel, then it implies that you are seeking and trying to control and wield power as a show of influence and stature over your friends.

Weapons

Gun

Distress and worries. Guns in a dream denote worries brought about by external pressures relating to people's opinions of you. If you killed someone, it means that you will lose respect from your peers, whereas if you saw someone else with a gun, it means that people with evil intentions will cause you worries and may even cause you sickness requiring medical help.

Sword

Protection. The sword is a symbol of strength and protection. You will be able to cut your way successfully through problems that you face at the moment if you have dreamt of the sword. However, if the sword is broken in your dream it means that you are trying to hide from current problems.

Bow and Arrow

Travel in the right direction. Arrows in dreams represent movement and our way forward: arrows act as a signpost, signifying the need for action. A broken arrow, however, is a warning that there could be difficulties in your relationship that need to be looked at.

Death

Death in a dream does not literally mean 'death', but refers to the closing of one activity and the start of a new one. It is in fact symbolic of regeneration. Often it means that there will be a complete change in your life, indicating the death of the past. You are going to give up all that you have now and go down a different avenue in life. So it's off with the old and on with the new.

Death's Hand

Age

Worry. To dream that you have aged indicates worry; it may also mean that you are feeling a bit down and perhaps should see a doctor. To see old people in your dream is a good omen; to see someone younger, or even a younger version of yourself, indicates that there is a need to take a fresh approach in the way you live your life.

Suffocation

Time for a check-up. If you dream of suffocation, it may indicate that you are having breathing difficulties in your sleep. You may simply be ill at the moment with a cold; however, this dream indicates that you need to check your health.

Hanging

You will be rewarded. This dream generally brings good news, providing that you are not the hangman in your dream, which signifies you will let someone down. You should also refrain from taking action against others.

Suicide

A need for relaxation. To dream of suicide means that you could be over-stressed at the moment and need to relax. It is perhaps a time to find someone whom you can share your feelings with. Should this dream occur, it may well be worth having a chat with a doctor or a therapist.

Bereavement

Frustration and sadness. A dream involving bereavement often indicates that you are worried about someone close to you. However, this dream also suggests that there will be news of a wedding or birth. If you do not receive this good news, then you are frustrated by business plans.

Morgue

Take care. If you dream of yourself in a morgue, then you may not be looking after your health: take this dream as a warning. Equally, if you see someone whom you know in the morgue in your dream, you should pay that person some extra attention and care.

Corpse

Sadness. Corpses in dreams bring disappointment. To see the corpse of your partner indicates that all is not well with the relationship. If you see the corpse of someone you know in a shop or your workplace in a dream, this indicates a major problem at work.

Embalming

Status loss. To see yourself being embalmed in a dream indicates that there is going to be a sudden status change for the worse. There is a need to prepare for this and make sure that you have adjusted your lifestyle appropriately. Embalming also indicates that your involvements with those lacking in ethics and values equal to those that you are used to will result in disgrace through false friendships.

Funeral Imagery

Funeral

Change. To see a funeral, or even your own funeral, means that you are very worried and stress is at a high level.

However, things are going to change for the better very soon. Like death dreams, a funeral dream means that you are going to be able to leave past problems behind.

Shroud

A period of distress and anxiety. The problems you are worrying about can be resolved if you take control and prevent others from running your business for you. If the shroud was lifted in your dream, this will tell you that you can reveal yourself to those around you in the business world. To see shrouded corpses indicates a sequence of material and emotional losses.

Coffin

Sadness if occupied, joy if not. To dream of a coffin with someone inside represents financial problems. It also means quarrels with someone close to you and therefore represents the death of a friendship. If the coffin is empty, you will make amends with someone over a dispute.

Bier

Losses. To see a bier (coffin stand) indicates a loss and could be a way of your intuition telling you of unfortunate news regarding a friend or relative. To see a bier with flowers in a church indicates the breakdown of a marriage.

Pallbearer

Achievement. If you dream that you are a pallbearer, then it indicates promotion and an increase in status. However, if you see a pallbearer in your dream, it indicates that you will upset a company or the local council.

Hearse

Promotion. If you dream of driving a hearse, it means that you will be rewarded with a promotion in your job, where you will take on more responsibility and be aided by others. If the hearse is drawn by a feathered horse, this indicates a marriage is near.

Cremation

Trust in others. If you see your own cremation in your dream, then you will be let down
by another person – the augury being one of self-reliance as the only way to your success.
To dream of another person's cremation indicates that you will receive some good news
inheritance-wise. If you did not know the person, you will receive a windfall of an
unexpected nature.

Cemetery

Prospects. Cemeteries in dreams have different meanings depending on how well the grounds
are kept. If the grounds are in a tidy condition, then there will be happiness and financial

rewards in the future. If the grounds look dreary, there may be trouble ahead, though news from friends will bring prosperity, resolving your problems.

Grave

Sad news. A grave in a dream represents sad news, although not necessarily death. A grave with flowers indicates a broken promise, while a grave in disrepair is said to indicate a broken heart. If you dream of someone digging a grave, then there are people around you who may not be all that they seem. Difficulties are set to cause problems for you.

Memorial

Show kindness. A memorial in a dream means that you will have to show patience and kindness to relatives who are likely to be going through a bout of troubles and sickness. This dream confers upon you the role of counsellor, so prepare to lend an ear.

Wreath

A celebration. If you dream of a wreath, it means that there is to be a celebration, perhaps even a wedding. If the flowers are fresh, it reveals great new potential for you to expand and broaden your horizons into new areas of interest and encounters with new people. Withered flowers, however, indicate regret and remorse in love.

Widow

If you are the widow in your dream, it denotes troubles through malice, envy and jealousy aimed at you, to undermine and bring you into disrepute. For a man to dream that he has relations of a serious nature with a widow indicates initial wish fulfilment followed by tragedy and loss of the relationship through the intervention of unseen fated forces.

Obituary

Good news. Reading an obituary in a paper in your dream signifies good news and can often mean you will receive news of a marriage. If you are writing an obituary in your dream, you may hear that an old lover is getting married.

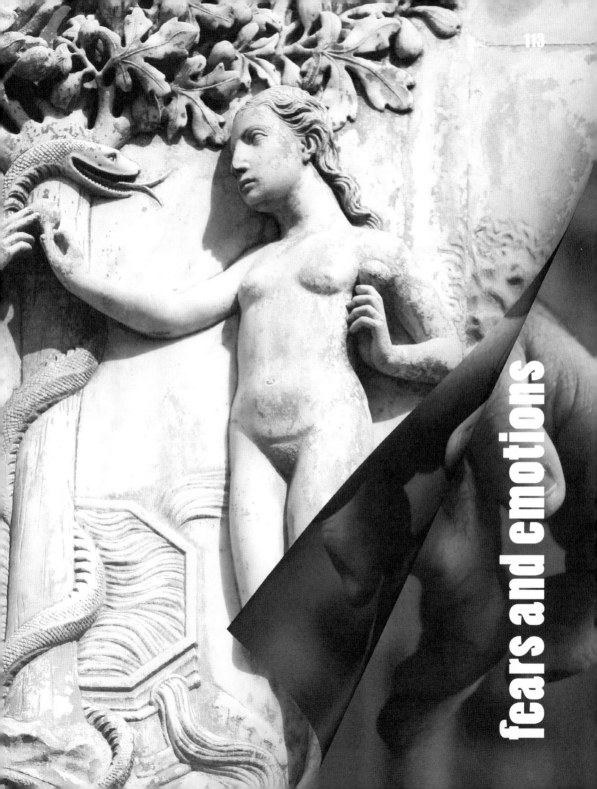

fears and emotions

Negative Situations

It is well known that dreams can be manifestations of our deepest fears and worries. Fear itself in a dream can anticipate dealing with that fear or obstacle in real life. Although negative situations in dreams can leave a bad taste in the mouth, they are not always what they seem.

Fear and Danger

Victim

Self-pity. If you feel that you are a victim in a dream, then it may indicate that you need to think about other people's positions, not just your own. Family problems are highlighted and indicate that it is no use just ignoring the issues but that you need to sit down with all the parties involved and sort them out.

Failure

Work hard. Dreaming of failure is your mind's way of telling you to keep on working at a project. If you stick at it, then you will succeed; you just need to put more energy into the situation. Regardless of whether this situation is to do with love or business, change your attitude, put the effort in and you will be rewarded.

Falling

Fear of failure. Falling in a dream is very common and represents a multitude of different fears, including fear of failing at business and sex, and also having to endure a lack of respect. The type of fall you experience in your dream determines the outcome. If you fall a long distance, then the changes you make in your life will take a lot of effort to go forward. On the other hand, if you fall a short distance, then you will be able to get over the setback quickly. If you are walking and you fall over in the company of others, then their friendship is not to be trusted.

To fall into water can represent financial stress, but to see others fall means that you will win the day.

Drowning

Emotional pain. If you dream of drowning, it is because you have a fear of your emotions at the moment. This is a time when you have to look at relationships very closely. This dream also indicates that you feel emotionally vulnerable in business dealings. If you managed to save yourself or someone saves you, then it is an indication that you will get the help you need to overcome the problems.

Isolation

Worries. If you dream that you are isolated, it means that you have complex and personal issues on your mind that you are having difficulty explaining to others. Perhaps if you tried to talk to your friends, you would find that they would at least listen and therefore share some of the pressure that you have been dealing with alone; they may even contribute towards sorting out the bones of contention.

Abandonment

Trouble. If you have dreamt that you have been abandoned, then you will find that over the next few weeks there will be a reconciliation with an old friend. If you dreamt that you abandoned someone else, then you will find that this is a warning not to be ignored or you could lose contact with that person. If you abandoned something you did not like in your dream, it signifies that you will be able to let go of it in real life.

Mask

Deception. To dream of someone in a mask means that you are being deceived. In real life, you may feel that this is true but do not know who the person is. When in a dream state, concentrate on seeing the person behind the mask.

Blindfold

Excitement and fear. The meaning of this dream is different according to the circumstances: if you were blindfolded, it is a way of testing yourself and your level of faith in others when there is nothing visible to latch on to but only words and promises. If you blindfolded others, it suggests a wish for anonymous affairs.

Trapped

A warning. If you dream about trapping an animal, then it means success in business and work endeavours. However, if you dream of being trapped or trapping another person, it relates to relationships that are fruitless to pursue. If you dream about feeling claustrophobic, then it is important that you look to other people around you. For instance, if you feel claustrophobic in your dream and you have a partner, then it indicates that perhaps you feel that you need a little time apart from each other.

Escape

Obstacles. A common dream indicating that you will encounter obstacles that you must try to overcome. If you escape from prison, then it indicates that you are feeling confined and trying to get out of a situation. Escaping from disasters, such as fires, indicates an anxious transformation with a successful outcome. Escaping from water means escaping from an emotional involvement. Escaping from animals represents escaping from people who are holding you down.

Lost

Find a new direction. If you feel that you are lost in a dream, it indicates that you feel you have lost your way in life. You are in a situation where you need to find a new direction for yourself. If you are on land, then it is likely to be a career direction, whereas if it is at sea, then it is an emotional direction. In the dream itself, whether you find a direction to go in, and how easy that is, will influence how easy it is to find a new direction when you wake.

Disgrace

Love issues. Fearing disgrace in a dream is more often than not related to love affairs. It is a fear that you will do something that will upset others or someone in the family. Treat it as an issue that can be looked at when you are awake to see how much of a worry it actually is. Most of the time, you will find that you have worried over nothing.

Humiliation

Arrogance. If you have a fear of being humiliated in your dreams, it is an indication that you may well be displaying arrogance at the moment and this is likely to lose you some friends. Take heed of this warning for it will prevent unnecessary errors due to vanity and pride; it will help you to see the real complexities involved in the situation and facilitate a successful outcome.

Laughter

Sorrow. If you are laughing at others in your dream, it indicates that you might have to deal with an unpleasant episode in the next few days. The exception is if you are laughing at children, which brings news of financial rewards. Also take into account the situation of where the laughter occurred; if the laughter seemed inappropriate, then you will not be laughing in a few days.

Teasing

Gatherings. If you dream of teasing someone, then it indicates that there will be a social party soon that will bring enjoyment. If someone is teasing you in your dream, then it indicates that there will be improvement in your life.

Hardship

Financial balancing. If you dream that you are in hardship, it suggests that it is time for you to sort out your finances, as money is starting to flow out quicker than it is coming in and credit card bills are likely to be piling up. The good news, though, is that these problems can be sorted out now before they get worse.

Temptation

Do not give up. Your strength of purpose is required at the moment, particularly as others may be trying to slow you down. This is a dream about perseverance and, if you resisted falling for temptation, then you will succeed in a worthwhile objective.

Enemy

Friends. To dream of enemies means that you are about to discover your true friends who will rally round and support you in your endeavours. If you are perpetrating hostility towards another, then this dream is a warning to hold back, as there is a great deal of missing information that will later reveal itself, showing that your friends are indeed loyal.

Revenge

Acceptance. If you dream that you have taken revenge against someone in your dream, then it means that you cannot accept your current situation and are unable to go forward. If someone is seeking revenge against you, then it indicates that you may have let someone down and so it may be time to make amends.

Arguments

Problem resolution. This type of dream allows your mind to look at your subconscious to enable you to analyse both sides of the problem. If you argue about a problem that you are experiencing in your life, then you will be able to resolve it when the morning comes. However, if you lose your temper in the dream, it indicates that you are trying to rush a decision.

Betrayal

Be aware. If you dream that you have been betrayed by friends, then it is a warning to look at the situation closely. They may not be trying to betray you intentionally but maybe things are not as clear as they should be. If you betray others in a dream, then this heralds that you may be contemplating deception as a means to an end. Think it through, for the repercussions will be dire in the end.

Reprieve

Time to act. If in your dream you have been reprieved, this is a warning for you to act now before it is too late. You will only get the time if you put in the effort to sort out the situation now.

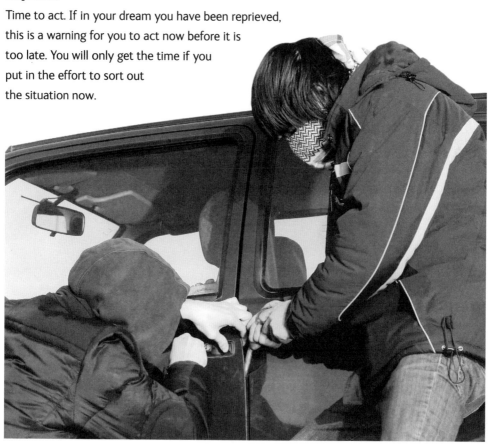

Crime and Law

Crime

Change of circumstances. If you dream that you are a victim of a crime, then it means a change for the better; you should receive something soon to boost your spirits. However, if you dream that you are committing the crime, then it is a warning to hold your tongue or you could do a disservice to a friend by speaking out of turn.

Robbery

To lose something. Oddly enough, if you dream of losing something of value in a dream, it indicates that unexpected gains are soon coming your way. If it is money that you have lost, it is a warning to try to curb your extravagant expenditure.

Rape

Reputation. As a dream omen, being raped or committing a rape warns you to be careful in a current relationship situation. This may not even be in a sexual situation; it is just that you could be taken advantage of and therefore need to be on your guard.

Homicide

Repressed anger. To dream of committing homicide is a warning that you are allowing yourself to react too quickly to events. It is a time to sit back and take steps to sort out problems that you have at the moment with friends or partner.

Police

Security. Police in dreams represent security and assistance. If the police are coming to your rescue, it means that security will be put in place to ensure that you do not run into problems. Even if you find yourself on the wrong side of the law, this is still a fortunate omen and leads to assistance being given to you.

Arrest

Obstacle. Being arrested shows that there is something that you need to sort out. The positive aspect is that the obstacle is a temporary block to your progress and once it is overcome you will achieve the desired results. To see others arrested means that you will gain promotion in your work situation.

Accusation

Warning. If you face an accusation in your dream, then it is a warning that there are some people around you who may not be acting in your best interests. The warning is that if you take action now you can protect and defend yourself so that the situation does not affect your interests.

Summons

Act now. If you receive a summons in your dream, it means that you have left something undone. Often this dream means that you have forgotten to pay your bills and is a warning to make sure that your paperwork is up to date.

Questioning

Reasoning. If you are being questioned in a dream, then this is a way of trying to get to the root of your problems. Your mind is assimilating the facts in your dream and when you wake you will have the answers before you.

Lawyer

Wasted money. If you dream of hiring a lawyer in your dream, then this is a warning not to waste money at the moment. If you dream of being a lawyer, this brings fortuitous news of money.

Courtroom

Optimism. Courts in dreams often relate to financial matters. There is a need to ensure that you are looking at long-term answers with regard to your life and not just short-term solutions. Courts indicate time and structure and that is what you have to focus on.

Jury

Use your intuition. To dream of serving on a jury is a message that you should rely on your own instincts and intuition to deal with a current issue. If you do, then you will get the right verdict. To dream of appearing before a jury indicates that you are about to receive a reward for all the work you have put in lately.

Witness

Avoid confrontation. If you dream that you are a witness, it indicates that you are holding information back. Nevertheless, you should not make a hasty decision and rush in, as the dream is warning you that you could make the situation worse.

Acquittal

Obstacles. Dreams of acquittal indicate that you are about to face an imminent problem that has some history attached to it. The obstacles that are ahead of you are surmountable, even though they seem impossible at the moment. Perseverance will lead to a successful resolution with an unexpected twist of good fortune in your favour.

Convicts

Escape. To dream of being a convict means that you are feeling tied down in a particular situation. The good news, though, is that this will not last for very long and soon you will be able to break free. If you dream that your partner is a convict, then you are worried that they have not been as open as you would like regarding their past.

Jailer

Lack of support. If you see a jailer in your dream, it means that a friend will let you down when you need them. Likewise, if you dream of jailing someone else, then, just when they need your help, you are likely to let them down, unless you take note of this dream and act to the contrary.

Jail

Obstacles. A dream about a jail represents obstacles that you are facing and need to get out of. If you succeeded in your dream to escape from jail, then it indicates that you will be able to extradite yourself from a problem in your life. The longer it takes you to get out of jail, the harder it will be, but you will overcome the situation.

Traits and Emotions

Negative traits and emotions are common in dreams, from laziness and jealousy to melancholy and anger – the heightened emotion of anger, for example, is often an indication that you need to calm down and work towards compromise with someone.

Character Traits

Laziness

Relaxation. If you dream of being lazy, then it can indicate that you have been working too hard recently and that you need to relax and take time out. If you dream that other people are telling you that you are lazy, then there could be an element of truth to their jibes.

Hatred

Beware of your responses. To feel hatred against a person in your dream is a warning that you are being too critical. If in your dream someone is issuing hateful vibes towards you, then you will find that friends will rally round to support you in any problems that you have.

Prejudice

If you are prejudiced against someone in your dreams, it indicates that you are not taking their views into consideration and this will have a detrimental effect on your success. If someone bears prejudice against you in a dream, then you will need to make more effort to explain your plans.

Jealousy

Problems. If in your dream jealousy concerns another person in a relationship, then you can expect problems in your relationship. If you are jealous of another person at work because of their career, then you are heading for career problems. If the jealousy is being directed at you, however, you will be able to turn the problem into an advantage.

Cheating

Your luck will change. If you dream of being cheated, then it means that there is some good news on its way to you soon, as something you thought you were not going to achieve will work out in your favour. However, if you dream of cheating someone else, then this is a warning that it is best for you to act above board otherwise your deception will be discovered.

Bragging

Warning. If you dream that someone has been bragging to you, then it may mean that you have to look closely at any business dealings that you are involved in with this person. If you are bragging in your dream, then it is important that in the morning you think carefully about what you have said to others; you may need to make some changes.

Admiration

Vanity. If you dream of being admired, then you have a need to take a closer look at your outward behaviour and examine yourself for signs of vanity that could mar and weaken the bonds of your friendships. To dream of admiring others means that help from your friends will soon spur you on the way.

Anxiety

No need to worry. Dreams are often a way of playing out fears and teaching you ways to overcome the situation. The outcome of these situations is always in the positive. Anxiety in a dream is actually presenting a contrary message: that you have the confidence and ability to go out and tackle a dilemma.

Pride

Pride comes before a fall. Showing pride in a dream about your own activities indicates that your plans may not work out and that others will undermine your work. However, if pride is shown by others, then this can indicate rapid progress concerning your career over the next few months.

Power

Achievement. Dreaming of being powerful is an indication that achievement is going to come your way. This dream is an omen not to give up now but to fight for your goals and continue the struggles. This is a time when you are harnessing your skills and talents effectively. Victory is very possible if you endure the road ahead.

Fame

Be realistic. To dream of fame is quite common and represents a fantasy rather than anything based in reality. This dream is therefore reminding you to make sure that you are setting realistic aims. If you dream of meeting someone who is famous, this means that you should persevere in your endeavours, for you will get help from an unexpected source very soon.

Emotions

Colours

Colours in dreams are very significant, as they give an indication of your mood with regard to how you and others react. The dreams will be modified by what objects feature and what actions are taking place, but the basics are:

 Blue: Gives calmness and a sense of spirituality; it promotes spiritual well-being and understanding; it is also a good dream for friendship and help from others. It means that people are around to help you with your ideas, offering emotional support and advice.

 Green: Brings luck and help in finances. It also brings love issues and fertility to the meaning of dreams. It is a good colour as far as financial negotiations are concerned and it means luck is on your side. Green is also ideal when looking at issues to do with the family, as it greatly enhances fertility and growth of the family.

Orange: A vibrant colour that promotes health and energy; it is a fast colour which means that, when orange is seen, changes will take place quickly. It is a colour of optimism and therefore the energy that you deliver at the moment will be rewarded in success.

Pink: Brings romance and affection but also honour and the honour of being looked up to by others. Pink is often shown at the start of a new relationship.

Purple: Represents career success and achievement. It also represents royalty and the church and therefore is often associated in dreams with forthcoming news of promotion or being honoured. It can mean meetings with important people who may be able to promote you in some way.

Red: Passion, love and also strength and anger. It is common in dreams when emotions are high. If you are wearing red in your dream, then you want to attract attention from another person, and if another person is wearing red, then they want you to notice them. Red faces can show anger and so caution should be applied with this sort of dream.

White: Purity and clearness. White means that everything will go well and that the choices you have taken are correct. It is also the colour of protection so that you will be protected and you will be protecting others.

Yellow: Brings strength of mind and determination; it is a colour of communication so is very good in business dealings and negotiations. Yellow is a good colour when connected with messages and the start of new ventures.

Magenta: Brings hope of new projects, as well as enthusiasm and motivation from others.

Cyan: Brings reflection and thought; it means negotiations will go well, as you will be able to sit down and discuss your options in a constructive way.

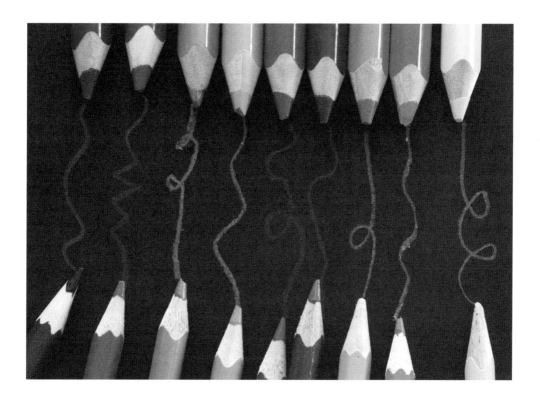

Indigo: In a dream, indigo means that you will have the authority of others to help you with your decisions; they will support you while keeping a tight hold on the reins.

Brown: Represents hesitancy and uncertainty and therefore in a dream can indicate events that need to be looked at carefully. You should be cautious. However, brown is also a colour that represents hard work to get the rewards that you want.

Grey: A neutral colour that can represent reaching stalemate. It is a message that things will take their time to sort out.

Black: An unfavourable omen, as it brings difficulties and obstacles to overcome.

If the colour is fluorescent, it brightly reflects whatever light source there is and in dreams this indicates that the effort you put in will swiftly be rewarded. If the colour is aglow in the dark, then it indicates that changes are already on the way.

If you see colours in your dreams that you would not normally see when you are awake – such as ultraviolet and infrared – this indicates that your perception is being opened and that you are able to perceive people's invisible issues rather than just the surface impressions. You will find that this will often give more insight into a situation when you are awake.

Fear

Conquering problems. Fear in a dream is a way of playing out a scenario; in this way you are able to work out a resolution so that when you experience the situation in real life you will be able to face it without fear. To dream of sorting out your fears means that you will overcome the obstacles.

Terror

Success. Being terrified in dreams is about learning to cope with the situation.

As you overcome the situation you will not be frightened any more; a successful outcome is assured. To see others terrified means that their terror will worry you and that you will help them by contributing towards bringing about a resolution.

Sadness

Worries will be over soon. If you dream that you are sad, then it indicates that you have friends who will help and support you. If someone else is crying, then you will need to go to their aid.

Melancholy

Sadness and failure. If you dream of melancholy in a relationship, then it indicates that there are problems with the relationship and that it will fail. In all events the feeling of melancholy in a dream indicates that the actions you are taking will not have the desired happiness that you wish for.

Anger

Compromise. If you dream of being angry with someone, then it indicates that they may have caused you a problem but you may be overreacting. Your assistance and input would significantly aid the situation and help resolve and finalize a difficult decision. Equally if you dream that someone is angry with you, then they are asking for your help.

Annoyance

Speedy fulfilment. If you dream of being annoyed about something or with someone, you will actually find that the next day you will no longer be annoyed. In fact, this dream bodes well for a pleasant, breezy day.

Apathy

Step up a gear. If you dream of being apathetic towards something or someone, then your dream is telling you to stop being a defeatist and to take up the challenge and continue with your objectives. To experience the apathy of others in a dream signifies that you may need to review your aims and not allow the despondency of others to discourage you.

house and home

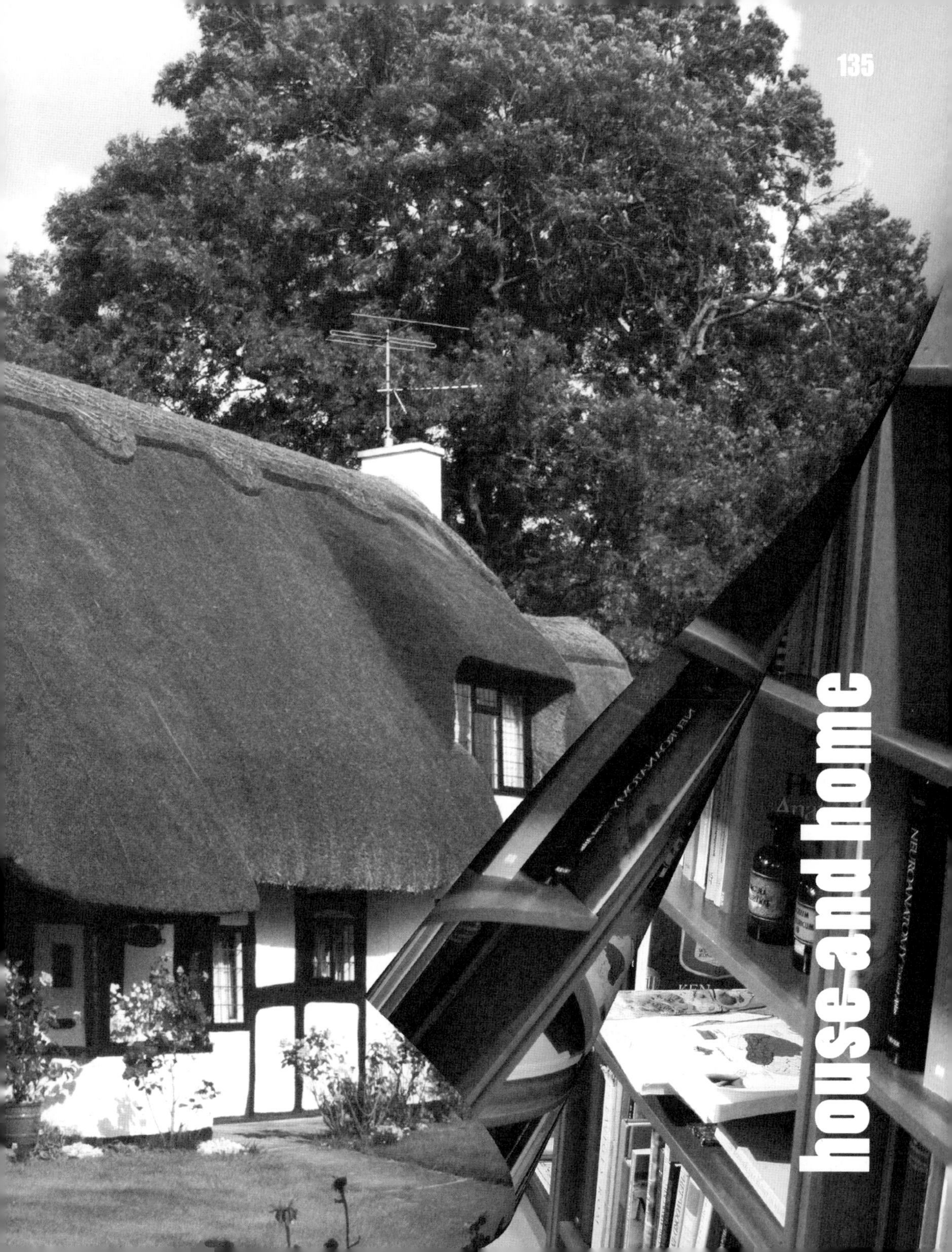

Home

Home means different things to different people – it may be the building in which we live or where our parents live, the area or where we came from. Dreaming of the home tends to mean satisfaction and suggests that you are content with the way things are. It indicates a wish to keep things stable in your life.

Domestic Matters

Tenancy or Rent

Mortgages. To dream that you are only a tenant or paying rent implies that you wish to move on and buy a place of your own. This dream can be taken as a sign that you are about to make a move and finances look good for long-term investments.

Mortgage

Financial pressures. Dreaming of a mortgage indicates that you may be having difficulties with your finances. This is a dream that should prompt you into action to sort these out. Additionally, such dreams can refer to borrowings that must be kept within your limits – whether from institutions or from friends.

Buying or Selling a Home

This is a dream which reflects your desire to move house. It can also occur, of course, when you are due to move and can represent an anxiety situation. Often this type of dream will occur when you are looking for commitment in a relationship or thinking of starting a family. To see an estate agent in your dream indicates that concerns about false promises and lack of commitment from a partner need to be addressed before hard cash is invested into joint ventures that have no longevity or solid foundations.

Lodger

Secrets. If you have a lodger in your dreams, it indicates that you have some secrets that you are trying to hide; public knowledge of these secrets might cause considerable embarrassment to friends and family. They tend to involve extramarital affairs.

Destruction

Dissatisfaction. If you feel that your home is under threat, then it indicates that you are not happy with the home life. If you fear violence in your dream, then it is an indication that your family life needs to be looked into fast and seriously. It is important that you do not act impulsively but that you do act quickly.

Buildings

Building

Structure. Buildings represent foundation stones of your life and so, if the building is well kept and strong, then you have a suitably stable structure in place in your life. If the building is falling apart, then the structure to your life is in decay and this can indicate personal or financial issues that need to be addressed.

Architect

Planning. An architect uses plans and this indicates that you will be using your skills at planning a way forward. It is a dream of success, providing that you pay attention to detail and ensure that everything is planned meticulously. Take note of whether the architect in the dream is a traditionalist or a modernist – this will help you to focus on the type of details that will construct the success for you.

Boarding House

Temporary entanglements. If you dream that you are in a boarding house, it suggests that sometime in the next few weeks you will have temporary residential arrangements and you will quickly move on to somewhere else.

Mansion

Changes in fortune. To dream that you are in a mansion means that you will need to look carefully at financial issues around you. It is possible that you will need to save money now to ensure a more secure future. To see the mansion in the distance represents the long-term financial goals you have set yourself.

Palace

Honour. To dream of seeing a palace indicates that you will soon be honoured by those around you. If you dream of living in a palace, however, it indicates that you think of yourself too much and perhaps set yourself unrealistic goals.

Castle

An Englishman's home is his castle. Castles in dreams are reflections of the home and the protection it affords. If the castle is solid, then it indicates a domestically stable and enjoyable time. However, if there are problems with the castle or it looks in a state of ruin, then it is a warning to sort out the domestic situation before the family crumbles.

Tower

Destruction and rebuilding. If you have a dream of a tower, then you are about to face a fairly difficult time. The signs are that you will find your life turns around and what was once important to you seems quite insignificant. Your priorities will change over the course of the coming months.

Farmhouse

Prosperity. Dreaming of a farmhouse is an indication that you will be prosperous in your work. The image of the farmhouse shows that hard work will bring its rewards and, though it may take a while and you will continue to have to work at it, you will be successful and comfortable in the end.

Thatch

Gossip. Dreaming of a thatched house means that there is gossip around you. If the thatch is breaking down or the wind and rain make it through the roof, an affair is implied. This is a warning to sort out a relationship before it breaks down irretrievably.

Tent

Financial issues. If you are in a tent, then it indicates that you will soon see an improvement in your finances, just as long as the tent does not collapse – which indicates the loss of investments and money through careless speculation. Erecting a tent or sleeping in one implies that you will soon be purchasing a new home.

Location

Village

Stability. A village in a dream is a bit like an extended family: it shows that there is support from others around you for whatever problems that you feel you are going through. Neighbours and friends will help you out in your hour of need.

Town

Commerce and opportunities. Dreaming of a new town could indicate a search for new work opportunities. If it is a town close to your own place of residence, then it indicates that you have got to get yourself out and about to take advantage of the commercial opportunities that are awaiting you on your own doorstep.

City

Change of location. To dream that you are in a different city indicates a possible change of location; much of the dream will depend on your own attitude to the city or cities involved, but it is normally connected with work decisions regarding the movement of businesses.

Island

Isolation. If you dream that you are on an island, then this represents a need for time to yourself to reflect on your circumstances. It may be that you have a number of issues that you need to address and need time to think. If you are rescued from an island, or manage to gain freedom through your own means, you will be able to overcome the issues.

Desert

If picturesque, dreaming of a desert can indicate a successful outcome to a problem. If a sandstorm is brewing, then it indicates many small obstacles that will cloud your judgement, hinting that by facing these you will ultimately succeed through sheer perseverance.

Mountain

Obstacles. Mountains in dreams represent obstacles to overcome. The higher and more difficult the mountain is to climb, the harder it will be to achieve your goals, but if you reach the top you will succeed. This is a dream about the need for perseverance.

Jungle

Warning over resources. If you are in a jungle in your dream, then it indicates that you feel you are trying to do too much. Your resources are low and it is important that you watch finances and take note of what other people expect of you. You could be running out of time and energy.

House Features

Both interior and exterior features of your dream house are significant. Details such as doorknobs, windows, gates and fences all have different meanings. Some might leap out at you in your dream – and these are the ones to pay attention to.

Exterior

Door

Regrets and opportunities. Closed doors in dreams represent lost opportunities. Open doors suggest new opportunities which may be worth investigating as they have the potential to yield the highest rewards for you. Going through multiple doors in your dream indicates that you will experience a series of opportunities.

Doorbell

News. Someone ringing your doorbell is bringing you news of an opportunity. If you dream of ringing someone else's bell, then it indicates that you are about to take them some important news.

Knocker

Financial risk. Dreaming of a door knocker suggests that you might be worried about finances. To knock on someone else's door indicates a meeting with them to discuss financial issues, or a new business opportunity that is about to be proposed.

Lock

Legal activities. If you dream of a lock, it indicates that you will have some legal activities to deal with. To pick a lock is a warning that you must not allow yourself to get involved in activities that you know to be dishonest or conducted in an underhand way.

Key

Solutions. Keys are very important in dreams, as they represent solutions to problems. To be given a key means that you will receive help; likewise, to give a key to someone else indicates that you will be helping them. Unlocking a door with a key can indicate that a new opportunity will present itself. If your key unlocks a casket, then this indicates sexual involvement with someone. If, however, you find a keyhole and do not have a key, it indicates something that is not meant for you – even more so if you look through the keyhole.

Window

A 'window' into your psyche. Windows in dreams represent a way of looking at a given situation. Windows represent the soul's desire. Opening windows means that you are inviting others to share in your happiness, whereas closing them indicates that you are trying to shut others out. Broken windows indicate that you feel insecure and climbing out through a window indicates a wish to find a new challenge.

Fence

Obstacles. Fences to climb over represent obstacles. They can also symbolize the barriers we put up to prevent other people getting to know us. Just as we fence our home off from others, this dream suggests that you may be putting up obstacles to others to avoid having to get to know them on a deeper level.

Chimney

Accomplishment. The taller the chimney in your dream, the more successful your accomplishments will be, just like the smoke signals of the North American Indians; smoke at the top of a chimney means a message is on its way to you.

Gate

The next step. A gate in a dream signifies the next part of your plan. It represents an obstacle, but one that must be crossed. If the gate is open, then the path ahead for you is clear; if closed, then it simply means that you will have to make more of an effort, but you will achieve the same results.

Roof

Security. A roof in a dream represents the security of home. If the roof is leaking, then it is an indication that all is not well on the domestic side. A dream of repairing the roof will soon bring money back into the household.

Ladder

The ups and downs of life. Ladders are very simple metaphors in dreams – symbolizing the trials of life:

 Climbing to great heights: The height of the ladder will represent how far you have to climb to reach your goal, and how easy you find the climb will indicate the degree of ease or difficulty you will experience in the pursuit of your ambitions.

 Achieving your goals: Getting to the top of the ladder indicates that you may also gain prestige and recognition: you have achieved your aims. If you are using a ladder to climb to the top of a house, it can suggest that you are about to obtain the house of your dreams. If the ladder is by office blocks, then it indicates the achievement of the top position in your workplace.

Fear of responsibilities: If you get to the top of the ladder and start to suffer from vertigo, it can mean that you are afraid of taking on the responsibilities that have been placed upon you by others. It can also imply that you are afraid of the dizzy heights of success.

 Pressure and obstacles: A ladder breaking in front of you means that you will be faced with an obstacle but you are able to avoid it. To walk under a ladder indicates that you will have to deal with extra pressure at work.

 Supporting a friend: If you dream of walking along with a ladder, then it indicates that you will be called upon to help a friend.

Interior

Wall
Structure of your domestic life. The walls of buildings in dreams indicate how you feel about the current situation. If the walls are fine, then you are secure, but if they are crumbling, your home life may be unsettled. If you are whitewashing the walls, then it indicates that your efforts to repair the relationship are not getting to the root of the problem, only papering over the cracks.

Stairs
Obstacles. If you climb up stairs, you are achieving minor gains in work and finance; if you are going down stairs, then it indicates that things are not going well. The fact that the stairs lead upwards to a sleeping area indicates emotional security in a committed relationship.

Fireplace
Contentment. A fire or fireplace in the home in normal circumstances can represent domestic bliss and happiness. However, if the home itself is on fire, then this is a warning of brewing family trouble. Prepare for some domestic truths to be exposed.

Coal

Security. Coal represents comfort and contentment. The brighter the coals glow, the more comfortable you feel.

Electricity

Energy in your life. Electricity in a dream represents the energy that is coming into your life. The brightness of the spark will dictate how quickly things will take off. If you dream of switching electricity on, then it indicates the start of a new project. Equally, if you switch something off, then it indicates the end of a project or relationship.

Gas

Warning. Gas appearing in a dream is a warning omen, hinting at scandalous gossip which may be about you. Seeing a gas man in your dream, or lighting a gas appliance, suggests that finances need to be watched. Gas explosions signify an urgent need to curb talk and act on the difficulties, both in your finances and relationships.

Rooms

Basement

If the basement is dry or well stocked with wine, this can mean a firm foundation to the other details in your dream. To find relics or treasures in the basement suggests that you have ancient wisdom and that you would benefit from digging it up and using it. To see rot or vermin in the basement indicates petty vexations that will destroy the foundation of your work if you do not attend to them very soon.

Kitchen

Social state. The kitchen in a dream represents how we feel about the current family situation. The newer, cleaner and more comfortable you feel the kitchen is in your dream, the more you feel happy about your family situation.

Lounge

Security. The lounge in a dream represents your home and your security. The more comfortable the room in your dream, the better you feel about your home situation. If the lounge feels crowded, then it is an indication that you wish for more time to yourself.

Bathroom

Inner emotions. Dreaming of being in a bath or a bathroom indicates that you are trying to unravel your emotional thoughts at the moment and you are probably in need of the time to contemplate. If the temperature of the bath is too cold, then it suggests that you are not sure of your feelings; too hot and you are not ready to plunge into the relationship, which may be too hot to handle.

Library

Knowledge. If you see a library in your dreams, it can indicate that you may be about to take up a new study or hobby. It also indicates that you are not content with your present circumstances and intend to change. To be inside a library heralds interests and hobbies that will involve going back to college or taking up a new course of education.

Attic

Aspirations. The meaning of this type of dream is dictated by your age. In the young it can represent the hidden mysteries of sex and therefore it can be a warning against rushing into things. In older people it can represent the aspirations of comfort and security.

Furnishings and Household Chores

Furniture in a dream represents the home and the state of the furniture will reflect the state of your relationships within the home. If you dream of newer furniture than you have, then it indicates that finances are about to improve. If the furniture looks shabby, then it can be a warning against being frivolous with your expenditure. All the furnishings and ornaments – not to mention signs of necessary chores – mean different things.

Furniture and Furnishings

Chair

News. To see an empty chair in a dream indicates that you will receive unexpected news soon of someone who would normally occupy that chair. To sit in a chair yourself means that you have to prepare something. A rocking chair means that you will benefit from the labours of others.

Sofa

Friendship. If you dream of sitting on a sofa or even just looking at one, then this is an indication that you need to have a heart-to-heart with a friend. It appears that you may be taking one or two people for granted.

Bed

New undertakings. If you dream that you are making a bed, it indicates that you will shortly have some visitors. If you dream of being in your bed, then it is an indication that you have been overdoing it lately and need some time to yourself.

Table

Hard work and effort rewarded. To dream of a table indicates that you are about to undertake hard work and effort but that it will be worth it in the end when you are rewarded for your diligence.

Carpet

Good luck. Providing they are new or are in good condition, dreaming of carpets is a good sign in relation to your income. If the carpets are threadbare, then it indicates that financial problems may become an issue. Oriental rugs or carpets suggest visitors from overseas.

Rug

Good luck. To dream of rugs – providing they are new or in good condition – indicates income will improve. If the rugs are threadbare or tarnished in any way, then it suggests that financial problems are now a priority and that you urgently need to attend to issues of immediate debt.

Cushions

Selfish. To dream of lying on cushions indicates that you could be acting against others' interests. To dream of making cushions suggests a forthcoming marriage. Damaged or ripped cushions imply small returns from a great effort in a long-term project.

Curtains

Obstacles. Curtains in dreams represent obstacles and dealings hidden from view. If you are able to open the curtains, then it indicates that you will solve the problem. Closed curtains imply that it may be best to leave things alone for the time being; do not indulge any confidence to anyone until the unseen dangers have passed.

Kitchen and Storage Items

Shelves

Knowledge. To dream of shelves, particularly if they have objects and books on them, indicates that you will shortly be taking up a new interest or study in a new subject. There is a wish to absorb new knowledge and the type of shelves, old, wood or new, will determine the type of knowledge you will learn.

Cupboard

Money issues. An empty cupboard is a warning to be careful of extravagance otherwise you could find yourself in serious financial trouble. A full cupboard indicates a family get-together and an enjoyable time.

Jug

Friendship. To dream of full jugs indicates fun times with friends that are inspirational and have a bias towards health and fitness, whereas empty jugs portend a new acquaintance who will generate sparks which will blossom into a whirlwind romance.

Tray

Good luck. Dreaming of carrying a tray means that you will come into some good fortune shortly, ushered in by your quick-wittedness and charisma, but do not drop the tray, as that indicates social embarrassment through a bad talk or presentation of significance that highlights the wrong points.

Glass

Celebration. Drinking out of a glass or a goblet indicates that you will shortly receive news of a celebration. If the glass is broken, then you are not happy with the situation.

Crockery

Domestic happiness. China indicates happiness in domestic circles. If it is broken, though, then it can indicate problems in the home that need to be sorted out, particularly issues relating to paternity and family trees.

Teacup

Social pleasures. Dreaming of teacups indicates a happy party, afternoon tea or morning coffee that you will be invited to, and which will result in a new friendship.

Cutlery

Domestic arguments. Dreaming of cutlery is a warning not to be impulsive or react too quickly to what others might say. A dream such as this indicates arguments around the home.

Bottle

Celebration. Dreaming of full bottles is a sign of celebrations and a party to come, with much merriment for all concerned. Broken bottles mean problems from which you need to disengage before serious quarrels break out.

Fridge

Coldness. If your dream includes a fridge, it is a representation of how you feel at the moment and may reflect a coldness felt towards your partner. That is, providing the blankets have not fallen off you in your sleep.

Ladle

Domestic happiness. To dream of a ladle means that you will be lucky in family life with plenty of children around you to keep you busy. This is a dream about your wishes for a family.

Kettle

Contentment. A boiling kettle indicates contentment within the family home. If it is broken, then there are financial issues affecting the family that need to be resolved.

Bedroom Features

Pillow

Pillow talk. If the pillows are dirty in your dream, it suggests that you are being unfaithful to your partner. Otherwise this dream simply means that you need to spend some time discussing personal issues with your partner.

Mattress

Comfort zone. If you are dreaming that the mattress is fine, then there is not a problem – you are comfortable with a situation. However, if the mattress is uncomfortable, then there are problems with the current situation and the augury is that you would benefit by saving for the rainy days ahead.

Blanket

State of mind or marriage. Bedclothes represent how stable you feel in your emotional situation. Care should be taken to look at the colours of the blankets and sheets, as this is significant. If you feel that the bedclothes are falling off you or are frayed and tattered, it means that the relationship with your partner is also suffering at this time.

Household chores

Servant

Contentment. Dreaming that you are a servant yourself hints that you may be asked to help someone else and you will gladly undertake that role. To dream of having servants of your own means that you need to watch your bank balance at the moment and curb expenditure on luxuries that you cannot afford.

Broom

A clean sweep. A broom in a dream represents sweeping away the past and ushering in the new. This often relates to home and relationships, where a new broom symbolizes the throwing out of the old. The exception is that of a witch broom, which suggests that others will mock your old-fashioned ideals.

Polishing

Working for the future. If you dream of polishing, it indicates that you will be rewarded for your efforts. The greater the depth of the shine, the greater the prestige you can expect to enjoy. To inadvertently dull the shine whilst polishing indicates that you have a tendency to shy away from success.

Ironing

Profitability. If you dream of ironing – whether man or woman – it indicates that a new enterprise will be profitable. If you scorch your ironing, then it is a warning to look out for someone else who is trying to take your place.

Cooking

Social state. Cooking in a dream represents how you feel about the current family situation. It indicates the growing and nurturing of a family and your satisfaction in that role.

journey

Travel

To travel in your dream is to achieve your results. If you dream of travelling, you are on your way to reaching your goals. Take note of the journey and the type of conditions, as these will give clues as to how fast and easy it will be for you to attain your desires.

Travel Basics

Voyage

Emotional success. A rapid and significant increase in your stature or financial standing is heralded in a dream featuring a voyage. The type of voyage and the destination need to be correlated for a full interpretation. To see yourself going on a sea voyage suggests the love and affection of those around you and the satisfaction you have in your personal relationship. Voyaging by air suggests a business increase.

Passenger

Success. You should find things becoming easier for you over the next few months as everyone else is helping to make sure that things go well for you. Sit back and enjoy the attention of others and make the most of a very enjoyable and co-operative time.

Tourist

Relaxation. To dream of being a tourist simply reflects a wish to be one, and probably suggests that now is as good a time as any for making holiday arrangements.

Accident

Warning. This can be a warning about a forthcoming accident and therefore it may be advisable to stay clear of long journeys for the next day or two. An accident at sea relates to emotional relationship issues; on land it signifies business issues. On the whole, this dream foretells dangers that should be avoided for the next two to three days.

Finding Your Way

Map

Finding a direction. You are looking for a new direction in life if you find yourself studying a map in your dreams, and it can signify a physical or emotional journey. The relationship will have a corresponding complexity to the map. How rewarding it will be is indicated in your dream by the ease or difficulty you experience in understanding the symbols of the map.

Compass

Finding a direction. Using a compass in a dream means that you need to set a new direction. It can indicate a difficult time, as you may have strayed off course. If your compass is pointing north, this can suggest that you have strayed but have found your way back to the right path. To see south implies your goals lie in the opposite direction to the areas in which you are currently engaged. West indicates your goals will be realized by looking back in time at an old pursuit. East denotes that you must face a future with changes that are modifications of your existing circumstances.

Signpost

Direction. Seeing a signpost in your dream is important, as it often shows something of significance and of which you should take note. Signposts appear when a new path is needed for fulfilment, and point the way to a new opportunity or to a different route in life.

Guidance

Help yourself. If you dream that you need guidance from someone else during your travels, it is a sign that everything is not quite clear in your mind, but if you allow your intuition to work you will find the right direction.

Road

Paths of direction. If you dream of travelling up a road – whether walking or driving – then it indicates that you will be making changes to your life. The straighter the road is in the dream, the easier those changes will be in real life. A bumpy road signifies obstacles that will hinder your progress.

Path

A path in a dream represents a journey that you have to take. The narrower the path, the more obstacles you will have to face. If you dream of stepping off the kerb, then it indicates that you are being distracted from what you should be doing. Stepping back on to the path indicates that you are back on course for your original aspirations.

Crossroads

Decisions to be made. If you dream of a crossroads, it literally means that you have reached a crossroads in your life. It is time to think carefully about decisions that you need to make and what direction you go in next. This can be a time of major change and turning points, so you need to think and reflect deeply on any decisions before you race off in any one direction.

Bridge

Change. Crossing a bridge in a dream is a sign of making a change for the better; it means that you are starting on a new venture and indicates positive action. The only issue that needs to be addressed is the state of the bridge; if this appears unstable, then you should take it as a warning that you are not yet ready to make that change.

Destinations

Foreign Lands

New opportunities or a need for a break. Visiting other countries in your dream represents new opportunities in both business and pleasure and is an indication that you have aspirations towards new adventures. Foreign people in dreams are always considered to be a good omen, suggesting that you will do well with overseas connections. You may not actually visit the country featured in your dream, but you will have an encounter with that country and its culture in some way. This dream implies the broadening of horizons and experiences. It tells you to persevere and you will achieve your wishes, although you need to make sure that you take it at a gentle pace.

Orient

A spiritual awakening. To dream of the Orient suggests a hankering after a spiritual journey. Your religious convictions may be changing at this point and you may take time to investigate other belief systems as well as your own feelings on the matter.

Horizon

Success. The horizon represents the future and your personal ambitions. To dream of a new horizon means that you will achieve success and peace. A distant horizon is more favourable, as it generally means your goal is more achievable, while a near horizon means that you have not left yourself enough time to plan

Hill

Obstacles and achievement. Hills in dreams represent obstacles to overcome. The general guideline to understanding this type of dream is that if you reach the top of the hill you will achieve your goal. If you give up halfway or try walking round the hill, then you are trying to avoid the problem. This will only compound the issue and it will return later if you continue to avoid it.

Travel Accessories

Passport

Remember who you are. Dreaming about a passport most obviously suggests impending opportunities for foreign travel. But it can have alternative meanings: if you dream of losing your passport, then it is a warning that you are not being true to yourself and that you may be hiding your real self from others.

Ticket

News. Dreaming of tickets is an indication of news: the tickets will indicate what is expected, and if it is travel, then it indicates that your travel plans may be delayed, but news of the re-arrangement will come soon.

Baggage

Forget the past. If you dream that you have a lot of baggage, it means that you have not been able to forget someone from the past and before you go on you need to consign that person to history. Maintaining an emotional attachment to them is preventing your development and stopping you making a new attachment, because you are looking backwards instead of forwards.

Transportation

A physical journey from A to B is not the only kind of voyage, of course – we can make emotional journeys too as we grow and develop as individuals, in our careers and in our relationships. One would expect journeys to feature heavily in dreams, as we know how symbolic they can be. For example, an aeroplane in your dreams suggests impending news and business opportunities from afar.

On Foot

Walking

Paths to tread. If you are walking in a dream, it indicates that you have a particular direction in which to go; the type of terrain and the ease with which you tread the path in your dream reflect the ease with which you will accomplish the results.

Running

Escape. If you are running in a dream, it normally means that you are trying to escape something in your current situation. The outcome of the running may dictate whether you can escape the problem, but often this dream is about the need to face the reality of a situation rather than avoid it.

Climbing

General success. If you see yourself climbing, it indicates progress towards a certain goal and you will almost certainly reach your target. How arduous the task will be depends on how difficult you find the climb, although perseverance will pay off in the end.

Air

Flying

New experiences. Flying in a dream is very common; it represents our ambitions and indicates a need for new experiences.

- **Going up**: If you believe that you are pedalling upwards, then it indicates that hard work is required to achieve your goals. If you have wings, then there are people to support you on the way and you will find a much smoother ascent to your ambitions.

- **Under fire**: If you dream of being shot at while flying, it indicates that someone else could be working against your interests.

- **Over buildings**: If you fly over buildings in your dreams, it indicates that you have ambition to progress in your work or change jobs.

- **Over water**: Flying over water suggests the desire for a new sexual relationship and this sort of dream is often at the start of a new relationship.

- **Floating**: Just floating means that you are content and want to sit back and enjoy life as it is now.

- **Into space**: Flying into space indicates that you wish to have some time to reflect on your emotional situation and that, although things are going well, you need to think about long-term objectives.

Aeroplane

News from afar. If you see an aeroplane or travel in one in your dream, it is a general indication of news and business opportunities from another country. If you fall out of the plane, or it experiences difficulties in the air, you should take it as a warning to watch overseas investments.

Airport

Business investments. If you dream of being at an airport, then it means that you will receive news from someone abroad. This dream often brings news of investments in business ideas.

Helicopter

Escape. If you dream that you are in a helicopter, then it indicates that you are trying to escape the current situation. This dream warns you that you should also think of the needs of others who have supported you in the past.

Parachute

Escape. Dreaming of a parachute indicates a wish to escape from constantly worrying about your career so you can indulge your ideas and imagination. Dreams involving parachutes can also mean that relationships will be under scrutiny; the way in which you land – on your feet, back or perhaps even crash-landing on to a canopy – can be seen as a measure of your success after the critical phase has passed.

On the Road

Wheels

Progress. Wheels mean progress and the faster they are going round in your dream, the faster the progress you are making. A broken or punctured wheel means delays and stagnation through lack of effort from yourself.

Driving

Take your time. Roads mean journeys and suggest life decisions. However, if you are driving in your dream, then you could be trying to push things too fast; it is also a warning against gambling. On the other hand, if you are a passenger and someone is driving you, then that is good news, bringing financial benefits and career advancement.

Bicycle

Steady progress. If you dream of riding a bicycle, then it indicates that you are making slow but steady progress towards your goal, although you may need to make a great effort to get there.

Taxi

Sudden news. A speeding automobile means that you can expect sudden news. If this vehicle is a taxi, then it indicates that other people are helping you along your path. To run out of fuel en route implies misplaced confidences that will lead to an embarrassing situation for you.

Limousine

A dream involving a limousine indicates that there are going to be people around you to help you and that you will achieve whatever goal you have in mind comfortably and will enjoy the journey. If you are the driver, though, then the work seems to offer luxuries to others more than it does to you.

Motorcycle

Freedom to reach the goal on your own. If you are alone on the motorcycle, then it indicates that you want to achieve your goal on your own. To have a passenger means that a partnership will yield the best results.

Bus

Steady but slow progress. If you are on a bus in your dream, then it indicates that you will reach your goal, but there could be many stops and starts before you finish your journey. To be the driver of this passenger carrier suggests that you know what the journey ahead entails and that you know the route – so relax and enjoy the scenic ride.

Caravan

This is a dream about taking time out to work out what is important to you and what can be consigned to the past. To dream that you are in a caravan is a wish for change and control in your life. Sharing a caravan site means that you are finding it difficult to decide what you want to keep in your life; you may be considering the lives of those around you as guidance for your new emerging tastes.

Stagecoach

Sexual indiscretions. To dream of being on a stagecoach indicates a romantic involvement which may not be appreciated by others. There is a need for caution, as you may obtain the object of your desire but at a high cost.

By Rail

Train or Railway Station

Progress in your career. If you dream of railways or travelling on trains, then your career is moving swiftly on. It bodes well for support from others as well. The only concern is that if you dream that you are at a railway station and miss the train, then it is an indication that you are going to miss the opportunity unless you make a move for it now.

Locomotive

Achievement. To be driving a locomotive means that you are well on the way to achieving results, although take care not to get carried away with early progress. If a locomotive plays just a cameo role in your dream, then expect a visitor who will further your career.

Subway

Emotional depth. To dream that you are taking a subway or underground train on a journey is an indication of a painful emotional duty that must be executed. It is not something you can avoid, for it has a convoluted history and the quicker you confront and deal with it, the better.

On Water

Ship

Business prospects. Ships or journeys by ship represent business opportunities and prospects. How rough the seas are will indicate how much work will be required for success. Calm seas herald easy success and rough seas difficulties ahead, requiring a great deal of tenacity and stamina. The greater the number of ships seen, the greater the success.

Boat

Relationship issues. If you are in a boat or a canoe then details of the river or sea must also be taken into account, as these represent your emotions. If you are alone in the boat or canoe, then it means that you feel you are alone in love. Where the boat is heading will indicate the place where you will find love.

Sailing

Emotional happiness. To dream that you are sailing indicates a very emotionally happy time for you, as long as the sea is calm. If the water is choppy, though, and the sailing difficult, then you have some emotional difficulties to overcome.

Raft

Sort yourself out. To construct a raft yourself indicates achievements through your own volition. To float on a raft suggests that your own lethargy will lead to someone else taking advantage of your efforts.

work and leisure

Education

Images related to school and education crop up in dreams however old we are, perhaps because those periods in our life were particularly formative and leave us with important memories. Dreaming of examinations is a classic example – indicating a fear of failure.

Elements of Education

School

Looking to the past. If you are not still at school, dreaming you are at school – particularly if it is one of the schools you attended – suggests that you are not letting go of the past. This is causing a problem as you are unable to move on fully until you lay the past to rest. Exiting the school or looking at it from the outside denotes that a windfall of some kind is coming your way.

University

Learning. If you dream that you are at university, it is often a reflection of a waking fear that you did not make the most of educational opportunities offered in the past. It can be taken as a signal to return to your studies in some way. For those involved in higher education, this dream heralds a time that requires focus and attention to detail. You need to correlate these details with other aspects of the dream to assess what you need to do in order to succeed.

Lecture

To impart information. Attending a lecture in a dream suggests that you are about to learn something new, but that you will not be particularly brilliant at this subject. Delivering the lecture, however, implies that you will achieve great success with the new skills or subject you are about to learn.

Examination

Fear of failure. To dream that you are taking an exam symbolizes a fear of failure. If you have exams coming up, this is a common dream and simply encapsulates your anxiety about them. If you do not have an exam coming up, however, it suggests that you are about to be tested: whether you pass or fail will indicate how successful you will be in dealing with this trial. Failing can simply be a warning that you are overstretching yourself, while success means you will face the obstacle without difficulty.

Certificate

Reward and honour. To receive a certificate suggests that you may be in line for an award. Such a dream also indicates that the effort you put in now will be repaid in the end. To simply see a certificate in your dream should be taken as a warning to nurture the acorns if you want to see oak trees grow.

Graduation

Success. If you see yourself graduating in your dream, it indicates success. To witness a graduation ceremony suggests there will be an increase in your social and business affiliations that will confer a higher status upon you.

Mortarboard

Success. To see a mortarboard either on yourself or on someone else in a dream indicates that you will be successful in your studies. However, if you find that the mortarboard is too small, it may mean that you have made the wrong choice in your studies and should reconsider. If the mortarboard is too big, you may need to try harder at your studies. If you are not the academic type, then this dream would indicate that there could be some financial gain if you embrace new responsibilities.

School Objects

Blackboard

The writing is on the wall. To see a blackboard in a dream means that something has already been decided; the wording on the blackboard will reveal more about what this might be. If you are erasing words from a blackboard, it suggests that you are trying to begin again, or 'wipe the slate clean'.

Chalk

A message for you. If the chalk in your dream is simply lying around, with no writing nearby, it suggests that someone is having difficulty in getting a message through to you; possibly because you are putting up some form of block. If the chalk has already written the message, read it carefully to get your answer.

Desk

Effort required. To see a desk means that you have your work cut out to achieve your goals on time. If the desk is small and the pile of work on it large, then it implies that you need to cut to the chase before time runs out. If the desk is large and the pile comfortably organized, then you have time to mull over the finer details.

Books

A record of your actions. Books represent the details of the things you have done and the things you have yet to do; they are a record of your life. Dreaming of books, therefore, represents the drawing up of plans. To see others reading in a dream indicates that you could learn from someone else's knowledge, thus enhancing your life plans.

Dictionary

Say what you mean. If you see a dictionary in your dream, it means that you are not explaining yourself properly to others; the consequent confusion could result in the loss of an important friend. You may also need to tone down what you are saying to avoid arguments.

Encyclopedia

New things to do. When you see an encyclopedia in your dream, it indicates a desire to break free from your current routine and do something new. This may perhaps mean giving up your job and embarking on a less lucrative but more rewarding career.

Pen

Message from afar. A pen in a dream indicates a message from someone who will soon be returning to your life. If the pen does not work, take this as a warning that you may be drawn into a situation that could harm your reputation. The colour of the ink is also significant: red can signify danger, although it is also taken to mean strength and determination; blue tends to indicate the truth and sensitivity; black can mean that you are being obstinate.

Pencil

Good health. Pencils in dreams represent good luck and good health. If the pencil has an eraser on the end, you will be given the opportunity to rectify a mistake from the past. If you are using a pencil in the dream and find that the lead keeps breaking, it signifies that stress is soon going to mount; prepare to curb your explosive temper.

Subjects

Art

To develop your creativity. Learning art in a dream should be taken as encouragement to indulge your creative side. If you are involved in a discussion about art, however, this means that promotion could be on the way as a reward for your creativity.

Reading

Literary endeavours. To dream of reading a book may be the mind's way of telling you to sit down and write a book; a dream of this nature often leads to literary success in some form.

Numbers

Numbers in a dream can predict your destiny and they are often considered the key to the future. Although they are generally regarded as lucky, bear in mind that numbers seen in a dream are just as likely to be your next gas bill reading as the winning lottery numbers. The following list shows common interpretations of numbers, as assigned by numerologists, and these definitions may affect your understanding of your dream.

 1 – New beginnings; events pertaining to the person having the dream

 2 – Intuition and balance; the partner

 3 – Activity, fertility and growth

 4 – Order and structure

 5 – Resourcefulness and drive

6 – Harmony and love
 7 – Investigation and contemplation
 8 – Authority and executive decisions
 9 – Re-assessment and planning

Mathematics

Problem-solving. Similar to anagrams, seeing sums or mathematical formulae in a dream suggests that you have problems to solve; solving them in your dream indicates success in finding a solution in your waking life.

Science

Be more practical. This type of dream can be misleading, as it can imply that you need to use and develop your mind and intellectual skills. In fact, dreaming of attending a science class, or undertaking scientific work, means that you should focus on skills using the hands more, such as art.

Work

If you dream of work, then you are actually foretelling a period of domestic bliss in which the people who surround you are prepared to help and support you. Offices in dreams may indicate financial success – or even romantic opportunities. Dreaming of yourself in an alien profession can have a multitude of meanings, depending on the dream career.

Work Basics

Employer

If your employer appears in your dream, then he or she is trying to tell you something at work. The mood in the dream will reveal what they have to say to you, but it is important to ensure that all work is up to date.

Employment

Unemployment. To dream you are happily employed could mean that things are about to change and unemployment looms for you. To dream of giving employment to others means that you could find that someone else gets the job that you were after.

Office

Romantic opportunities. To dream of a busy office augurs well for finance. Strangely enough, romances can also flourish with dreams of offices. This is particularly true if the office in your dream is one that you are not familiar with.

Typist

Progress. As long as the typewriter or computer that you are working on in your dream is working, then you are able to make progress in your life. A jammed or broken typewriter suggests there are obstacles in your way. To dream that the keyboard on the computer keeps jamming and you have to reboot the computer indicates that something you have started is not finished and you will not be able to move on until that is complete.

Envelope

Concealed message. Receiving a letter is a direct message from your subconscious or from someone trying to communicate with you, but if you just see an envelope, it signifies that there are obstacles to be overcome before a situation can be resolved. An open envelope indicates that the problems will be easier to deal with than you think.

Letters

Messages. Letters in a dream at their most basic indicate that you are about to receive a message. If you see a letter of the alphabet, then it is shorthand for a word or a person; they may have that letter as the first letter of their name, for example.

 Receiving: To receive a letter is good news, as it brings a message from someone close to you. In your dream the letter may indicate extra information if you can read it. If the letter brings problems, then it may bring a struggle in waking life. If the letter is from a bank, then this would indicate financial difficulties that need to be resolved.

 Sending: Sending a letter means that you need to get a message over to someone. If it is a friend or a relative, then it can mean that you are having difficulty explaining to them something that is going on. A letter being sent to a partner can reveal frustration in your relationship; it can also indicate emotional or sexual problems which can be difficult to discuss with each other. In this case, the dream is suggesting that you approach your partner and talk about the problems before you drift even further apart.

Writing: To write love letters to unknown people may indicate that you wish to inform someone about an affair that you regret. By sending the letter in your dream, you feel that you have confessed and will not need to actually confess when you wake.

File

Put your life in order. If you dream of files, it means that you may have some filing of your own to sort out. Finances and business can be difficult around this time. Such dreams can also signify unexpected interruptions in business which can leave you feeling out of control.

Accounts

Financial worries. Dreaming of accounts or accountants often means that you are troubled by financial issues, or that your accounts need to be sorted out. It is a warning not to overspend or invest in things that you cannot afford.

Occupations

Book-keeper

Encountering a book-keeper in your dream is a warning to get your accounts in order. It may mean that you have one or two financial worries, but the purpose of the dream is to force you to address these sooner rather than later.

Teacher

Learn and teach. The presence of a teacher in your dream is an indication that you need to pull your socks up and do better. If you are the one doing the teaching, then you have some knowledge that you wish to pass on to others.

Janitor

Problems with children. If a janitor appears in your dream, regardless of whether it is you or somebody else, it indicates a problem with children that will need to be sorted out. Lots of little things are annoying you at the moment and are preventing you from making long-term plans. This dream is warning you to look at long-range goals and leave some of the smaller things until later.

Artist

Disagreements. An artist in a dream signifies a disagreement with your partner. You may also be going through a time when you are reconsidering your options. For those involved in creative endeavours, the direction of your research and indeed commentary may well come from the artist or type of artwork that you see in your dream.

Conductor

Guiding people. If you dream you are a conductor on a bus, then it indicates that soon you will be helping someone find their way in life. If you dream you are conducting an orchestra, then you will be helping someone develop their creativity, although this will not be without some difficulty.

Hairdresser

A sign of your health. If you dream that you are visiting your hairdresser (particularly if you are a woman), if you are pleased with the result, it indicates healthy times. For a man, a visit to the hairdresser may mean an indiscretion with a female. If you dream that you are the hairdresser and that is not actually your profession, then this is a request for help from someone.

Engineer

A person to aid you. To dream of an engineer means that you will need and receive the help of someone soon.

Mechanic

Help available. If you dream of a mechanic, then it indicates that soon someone will help you with your problems.

Plumber

Bladder problems. A reference to waterworks like this in a dream is an indication that there are physical problems that should be checked out.

Blacksmith

Long-term advantages. If you see a blacksmith in your dreams, it is a hint that the hard work you are undertaking now will be rewarded in the long term. If the smith shapes and fashions his metal with ease, it indicates that your success will astound others as well as yourself.

Carpenter

Enjoyable time ahead. A carpenter in your dream is considered to be a very lucky symbol: it shows that your endeavours will reap rewards. The nails will indicate how hard you have to work to achieve your aims – the larger the nails, the harder it will be. The strength with which the carpenter is sawing represents how hard you will have to work. It is also an indication that you will be able to saw your way through your problems. The carpenter's plane will indicate how smooth the trip will be.

Mason

Brotherhood. To dream of seeing a mason (regardless of whether it is a freemason or an artisan working on a building) simply means that there are people around who will help when you are in need.

Apprentice

Hard work. To dream that you are an apprentice signifies that you will need to work hard to gain the respect of others. Such a dream can also suggest that there are new, practical methods that you need to learn, and that you would benefit from honing your observations for maximum success.

Inventor

Achievement. To dream of an invention or being an inventor indicates that you will achieve great success. To meet an inventor means that you will find associates to help you in your unique endeavours. If you are the inventor yourself, then a phase of extraordinary thinking is about to elucidate an answer to a particular enquiry.

Tools of the Trade

Machinery

Anxiety but success. To see any form of machinery in a dream indicates anxiety, regardless of whether you work with that machinery in real life or not. However, the dream is positive in that it suggests that there are people around to help alleviate your concerns.

Engine

Friends to aid you. To dream of an engine – regardless of the type of vehicle it drives – signifies that there are many friends around you who will help in times of trouble. A disabled engine may bring misfortune and illness for someone close to you, or it may simply be your subconscious telling you that you have left the car lights on and are in danger of draining the battery.

Scales

Important decisions. Scales are an archetypal symbol and refer to the weighing up of ideas and making decisions. Seeing scales in a dream can also be about achieving the right balance between your needs and the needs of others. The scales can point to a legal matter as well, so it can act as a warning to avoid parking and speeding tickets.

Tape Measure

Start making plans. To dream of a tape measure means that you need to revisit plans that you may previously have made. It could also mean that you have underestimated costs on something you are about to purchase or that family members are in need of new clothes.

Anvil or Cobbler

Increase in wealth. If the anvil is working or the cobbler is mending shoes, then it indicates all is well and financially things will improve. However, if the anvil is broken, then this is a sign that there are financial problems to be sorted out.

Grindstone

A friend to help. If you dream of sharpening your knife on a grindstone, then it signifies that someone will help you in your endeavours. Nevertheless, hard work is involved and you will have 'your nose to the grindstone'.

Spade or Shovel

Work hard. If you see a spade in your dream, it means that you are about to embark on a lot of hard work. You will need strength and perseverance for the task and to be willing to take up the challenge. If you do, you will get the rewards that you deserve.

Axe

Cut through the confusion. Dreaming of an axe means that you will have to force your way through the confusion that surrounds you at the moment. However, you have the determination and will do well. In order to achieve this success, though, you must be clear in your goals.

Pump

Obstacles to which you hold the solution. Regardless of what type of pump it is – even a bicycle pump – this dream means that you hold the key to a problem yourself. If you are pumping away and there does not seem to be any progress, it means that you will have to push harder in your work. Dreaming of an oil well pump will bring rich rewards in the long-term future.

Music

Music affects our emotions and in a dream adds to the atmosphere, just like in a film. The type of music you hear in a dream will denote the general backdrop mood of the action. A happy, cheerful tune will inspire a happy, cheerful outlook whilst a dark melancholic tune will suggest sadness. Look up the instrument that you have dreamt of in this book to interpret your dream fully.

Instruments

Guitar

Appreciation. It is quite common to dream of playing a guitar, perhaps as part of a rock group. More than anything, this dream reveals a desire to be appreciated. Playing a guitar is also coupled with the wish for a sexual adventure and might indicate a period of passion.

Violin

Harmony. If you hear a violin in your dreams, it denotes a peaceful time. However, if the strings break or the sound is unbearable, then you have quarrels at hand to deal with.

Harp

The progress of time. If the strings of a harp break in your dream, this indicates that you want to stop time in your relationship; maybe you feel that you cannot continue in the relationship and that it is time you broke free from your partner. If the harp carries on playing in your dream, you have the ability to stay the course.

Flute

Domestic issues. To hear a flute being played in your dreams means that you are happy with

your domestic arrangements. However, if you are playing the flute, this means that you could be involved in an embarrassing situation.

Trumpet

Surprise. Playing or hearing a trumpet means that you are about to get an unexpected but welcome surprise, which usually reflects a significant and long-awaited achievement. Trumpet fanfares indicate a personal achievement that will make your heart glow with joy. Well done, you owe this success to your own uniqueness.

Drum

Success. To hear drums in your dreams indicates that news of success is on its way. Just as drums were used in Africa to carry messages before the advent of telephones, the drums now signify a message on its way to you.

Piano

Success. To hear or play a piano signifies success and enjoyment, providing of course that the piano is played in tune. If it is out of tune, then there is discordance within a relationship.

Accordion

Relief from sadness. If you dream that an accordion is playing, this means that, although you are sad at the moment, things will get better, as there will be joy in your life shortly.

Organ

Weddings and children. Organs are associated with the Church and therefore tend to signify a family gathering at a church. The type of music will determine what the celebration is for. A pleasing tune played on a musical organ can often symbolize sexual potency and the ability to attract members of the opposite sex, so fertility and relationships are often highlighted following a dream involving this old relative of the piano.

Performance

Singing

To sing by yourself is to want personal recognition. This dream indicates that you feel you are not being appreciated by those around you. To sing in a group indicates that you are likely to be feeling very fragile after a party in a few days.

Serenade

Romance. To dream of being serenaded – or you are serenading someone – shows that a romance has started and will blossom, providing, of course, that the person does not throw a bucket of water over you.

Concert

Good news. This dream is often a sign that you want to be involved with the person or group performing in the concert, indicating that you want to be part of their creativity. If you dream that you were taking part in the performance, it signifies that you would do well to put your talents on display, as they will be received with applause.

Orchestra

Friends and joy. Whether you dream you are listening to, playing in or watching an orchestra, the symbolism is the same: you have something to look forward to, involving a group activity that will bring you great personal pleasure.

Recreation

Sport and all sorts of pastimes and entertainment can symblize much in dreams. Games in general, for example, can represent achievement. If you dream of pleasure, it means that you are going to have the time to enjoy the rewards of all the hard effort you have put in recently. It is a sign that a relaxing and pleasurable time is on its way.

Games

Toys

Reliving your childhood. If you are older in years, then this dream indicates a desire to regain your younger years. If you are single and would like to have children, then the toys are a way of recapturing those innocent carefree days.

Dominoes

Caution advised. If you dream of seeing dominoes but do not actually play the game in your dream, you should be cautious; any purchases that you wanted to make should be delayed. If you are actually playing with the dominoes, it indicates that you have already taken a risky gamble, in which case it is time to retreat, as you are not going to win.

Chess

Strategy and political movements. Chess is one of the oldest games, originating from China. Just as chess can be a complicated game, you will need all your powers to manipulate events around you; there are political matters that need to be sorted out at work. If you win in your dream, then you should win in the real situation that faces you. Even if you lose, you can still win in real life, but you will have to change your strategy. You may also have to adjust your social life, manoeuvring your position and playing the game.

Dice

A gamble in life. For a woman, this implies a romantic gamble but there are many risks and dangers attached. 'Think again' is the message of this dream, especially if the pips show very low numbers. For a man, it implies gambles in large business ventures. But, unless you throw sixes, this is a dream of great loss to you personally. To throw winning streaks in a dream indicates a large windfall but not significant enough in size to change your lifestyle.

Cards

Your destiny awaits. Your destiny is laid out – if you can remember the cards that you saw, it is important to write them down once you have awoken. The Ace often represents the start of a new project; to see Hearts represents love, while Diamonds represent financial issues. Clubs represent strength and perseverance, and Spades represent obstacles.

Gambling, Money and Fortune

Money

In your dreams, money is a way of indicating reward. To give money to others in need indicates that money will come to you in a positive way. If you receive money for hard work, then it suggests good news and that you will be rewarded. Dreaming of receiving money, however, does not necessarily mean a financial reward. More often than not, dreaming of receiving money is an indication of emotional security.

- **Lottery**: Dreaming of a pools or lottery win does not necessarily foretell good news. In many ways, this can be seen as a warning not to squander, as money problems could haunt you in the near future.

- **Changing money**: If you have paper money in your dream and it turns into coins, then this is an indication that you will have problems but they will not be large. Changing money for foreign currency implies that a windfall will come your way.

- **Borrowing**: To borrow money in a dream is a warning that you need to curb your expenses and tighten your belt. Seeing your bank manager in a dream is not hopeful either and again indicates a need to watch your expenditure.

- **Stealing**: Stealing money in your dreams can actually be a good omen, as it indicates that you will receive an unexpected gift. Saving money or putting the money in a safe or bank means that you will be financially comfortable in the long term.

- **Receiving**: To receive rare coins in a dream is to be given an unexpected opportunity. To receive gold coins means that, although you will not be rich, you will be emotionally very happy. To receive small denominations of coins such as pennies or cents will mean that you will succeed financially in any major investment or business opportunities that are around. If the coins are all copper, then you will do well; if the coins are of silver, then not so well. To dream of a large number of gold coins means that the stock exchange may well have a major fall in value.

Forgeries: If you receive forged notes or counterfeit coins, then you are likely to fall ill soon. Also, if you receive a bundle of notes, then it promotes health and if you have been under the weather lately, then your health is going to improve.

Finding money: If you are male and you dream that you have found money and you are trying to hide it but cannot find a place, then it means that a woman will be the cause of a financial loss for you.

Holding money: If you dream that you are holding some coins in your hand, then this is a dream about the need for security and would indicate that you will soon be purchasing a house and taking out a mortgage.

Betting

You are about to take a gamble. It has been recorded that certain people who have dreamt of placing a bet, on a racehorse for example, have gambled the following day and have indeed won some money. You have to be careful, however, as this type of dream is not always necessarily a premonition. More often than not, this type of dream refers to a gamble that you are taking in your business life.

Winning

Achievement. If you dream of winning, then you are seeking recognition. If the win is in a team event, such as football, it reveals that you want to mix with others and be with a crowd.

Auction

Successful outcome. To dream of auctions indicates success and you will find that financially there is a bonus for you. In any business dealing, you will find that you get a fair price and negotiations will be pleasant.

Treasure

Profitable work. To dream of finding treasure means that the effort you have been putting into work recently will result in success. This may not simply be about money, but can also be success in anything you are putting effort into at the moment.

Pastimes and Entertainment

Kite Flying

Flying a kite represents your hopes and ideals. Whether you fulfil these goals depends on the way that the kite is flying in your dream: if the kite is soaring high in the sky, then you will be successful. However, if you are unable to launch it into the sky, or if it continues to crash, then fulfilling your hopes and dreams will be problematic.

Angling

Keeping your integrity. Angling indicates that you would be wise to hold true to your values, ethics and principles, especially where financial concerns are tied up with emotional issues and partnerships. The type of fish you are angling for will clarify in which area of your life you must hold fast to your vision. The type of fish may give further enlightenment to this dream.

Photography

Photography represents deception in dreams. If you dream a photographer is taking a picture of you, it indicates that you are about to get yourself and others into trouble unwittingly. To dream that you are taking the picture indicates that you will know about the person(s) who will cause your future prospects harm.

Television

Don't just watch, take action! This dream is telling you to take a chance on your dreams and hopes. Too much of the time you are acting as a spectator and are not taking control of the situation; it is time to make your own judgements and activate your ambitions.

Radio

Communication issues. Radios represent difficulties communicating with loved ones. This is particularly true if the radio reception is hazy. The dream is literally speaking to your wavelength and is telling you to buck up your ideas and communicate with loved ones, especially if there has been some distance between you, either through time or geographical residence.

Acting

Assertiveness. To dream of being or meeting an actor or actress heralds a period of forcefulness and determination on your part to assert yourself if you want to achieve your ambitions. But be warned not to repeat anything placed in your confidence, as you will lose more than just a friend.

Theatre

To see yourself acting is a wish fulfilment dream, unless, of course, you are an actor, in which case this could simply be your internal way of rehearsing and acting out the scenes before the performance. On a negative note, this dream can mean that you are trying to achieve status by upholding false pretensions. So stop acting and face your truth before you get yourself in too deep.

Dance

Dancing symbolizes transformation. People nowadays still use dance as a way of communicating with the higher spirits, such as the Dervishes of Islam, or the Native Americans in their rain dances. To dance is our body's way of trying to get in touch with our inner spirit. Dancing indicates joy and excitement at new prospects; it also represents a sexual awakening, indicating that romance is in the air.

Comedy

Temporary escapism. If you dream of a comedy, then it indicates a little light relief is on its way to you.

Gallery

Contentment is on its way. To dream you are wandering through an art gallery means that a period of peace and contentment will soon be with you, which will help you to relax. The pictures you view in your dream will give you an insight into the areas of your life that you need to escape from. However, if you are involved in the visual arts, or are in the process of investigating a creative idea, this dream strongly implies that the artists you are drawn to in the gallery will hold the key to your creative unfolding and even direction. Therefore, seek further information on the artists under review.

Carnival

A celebration. Generally, dreaming of a carnival indicates that you will receive good news in the form of a celebration. The exception is if the people at the carnival in your dream are masked, as this could mean that you are open to deception but cannot see it.

Fireworks

Fireworks in your life. Fireworks can represent a celebration or passion in a new relationship. Also, this type of dream can mean that you will be involved in heated arguments with others. Much depends on the other issues within the dream.

Sporting Activities

Race

Perseverance against time. A race indicates something that needs to be finished: you may lose out if you do not complete what you have started. If you win the race in your dream, then you are likely to win and achieve your goals in reality very soon.

Rowing

Winning the heart of a special person. To dream that you are rowing means that there is someone special in your life who you are striking up a relationship with. This will go well unless you capsize the boat in your dream, losing that love to another person.

Swimming

Inner emotions. Swimming represents getting in touch with your deep subconscious. The surroundings in your dream will be of importance: for instance, to swim at sea indicates greater luck than swimming in a pool. To swim nude denotes success in your current endeavours, whereas swimming with clothes on means that you are not letting others get emotionally close to you.

Diving

Establishing your feelings. Diving into water in a dream is a way of diving into your emotions. The clearer the water, the clearer your feelings. If the waters seem murky, and you are unsure of yourself, this indicates emotional distress at the moment. If the water is clear, then you are diving into a situation that will bring you happiness and an enjoyable sense of stillness as you ponder and rediscover yourself.

Football

A windfall expected. To dream of playing football is generally good news as it signifies the possibility of a financial gain. However, to be stuck on the reserves bench means that you need to be choosier with friends.

Cricket or Baseball

A long wait. To a certain extent, dreaming of cricket will be influenced by how you feel about the game. If you are in a cricket team and you win the match, you will feel that you have achieved something; the dream indicates a gathering of friends. If you lose, you are scared of letting your friends down. If you are watching the game, you need to relax at work to avoid things getting on top of you.

Boxing

Overconfidence. Whether you win, lose or are just watching a boxing match in your dream, the same meaning applies: your levels of confidence are too high. You need to be careful of this, otherwise events could turn against you if you do not weigh up the situation and the opposition carefully in advance.

Golf

Romantic affairs. Even though golf is quite a solitary game, in dreams it represents a new romantic liaison. To putt a hole-in-one would imply immediate and mutual reciprocation of love. To struggle but eventually finish the round implies time is needed to develop the bonds. To find yourself in the bunkers of the course implies an overzealous nature and carelessness in your approach, so think before you drive the club.

Gymnastics

Take care. Seeing gymnastics or exercise in your dreams indicates a need to be careful and not to overdo things; not necessarily from an exercise point of view, but in life in general. You are trying to do too much at once and are acting too impulsively.

relationships

Family

Unsurprisingly, the people closest to us will feature in our dreams. Dreaming of the family as a whole can mean many things, and interpretations depend upon the expressions on the faces of the individuals. If they are largely happy and smiling, it suggests that all is harmonious in the family at the time.

General Family

Children

Support. Parents never stop worrying about their children and so it is important to realize that most dreams involving your children are simply reflections of waking anxieties. If you hear your child calling you in a dream, however, it may be that they need your help in some matter.

Cousin

Arguments. Cousins can indicate arguments, often over the matter of an inheritance. Dreaming that you are romantically involved with a cousin means that family arguments of a different nature are about to erupt.

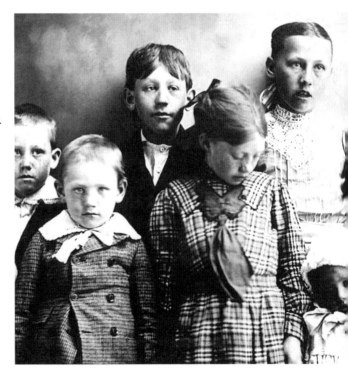

Parents

Support. Generally, parents appearing in a dream symbolize support: they are there for you and it is a message that you can go and talk to them about your difficulties and they will help you out as much as possible. If they talk to you in your dream, it is important that you listen carefully, as this message may be the clue to the resolution of the dream.

Grandparents

Advice. In most traditions, grandparents are considered fountains of wisdom and knowledge. It is important if you dream of your grandparents, as they are giving you a message that should be acted upon. If your grandparents have passed away, then it may indicate that they are contacting you as a spirit or ghost.

Guardian

Financial help. If you dream of a guardian, then it indicates that this person is willing and able to offer you help in your current situation. You must make the first move, though, and contact the person you see as the guardian to ask for help.

Men

Father

Support. A son dreaming of his father is in need of advice in business and finance, as his work may be experiencing financial difficulties. A daughter dreaming of her father is in need of help in an emotional matter and wants him to either approve of or help her in her current relationship.

Son

Pride. If you are a father and you dream of your son, then it augurs well for any business dealings. For a mother to dream of a son indicates that she is very proud of him; however, if you hear him calling, then he is asking for your help and may be in some despair.

Brother

Support. For a man, dreaming of your brother indicates quarrels, while for a woman it suggests long-term support and security. A dream involving solidarity between brothers indicates financial stability.

Uncle

Arguments and support. Often the nature of your relationship with your uncle will change what the dream means. To dream that your uncle is dead means that you have strong hostile opposition. To dream of arguing with an uncle indicates an unpleasant bout of illness that will befall a family member.

Nephew

Working together. Generally, dreaming of a nephew means that you will have an opportunity of working together in the near future and that this will be a fruitful time for your business. You should be careful to draw up boundaries, however, to make sure that the work falls to both of you equally so one party does not feel that they are being taken advantage of.

Husband

Contentment. To dream of your husband if you are married shows contentment in the relationship. However, if you dream of a husband when you are not married, it means that you are about to fall out with your partner, particularly if the relationship has just begun.

Women

Mother

Emotions. Your mother calling to you in a dream can indicate that you feel you are not doing enough to help her or paying her enough attention. Otherwise a mother represents the emotional security that perhaps you need at the moment.

Daughter

Support required. A mother dreaming of her daughter indicates a forthcoming argument, whereas a father dreaming of his daughter is more likely to find himself sorting out an emotional entanglement from which the daughter wishes to extricate herself.

Sister

Emotional support. If you are a woman and you dream of your sister, it could mean you are heading for an argument. However, if a man dreams of his sister, it means that she is there to help him with an emotional problem.

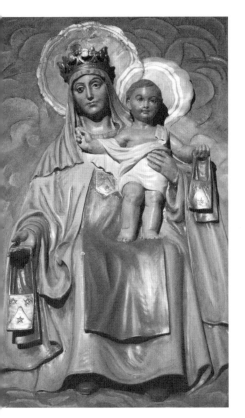

Aunt

Help. Much of the meaning of such a dream will depend on how close the relation is to you, but in general dreaming of an aunt means that you will receive help in sorting out an issue that involves a third party. It is possible that this issue is one relating to your family.

Niece

Worries. To dream of a niece is a warning to give this person a call and make sure they are all right, as often you will find they may need your help. In the long term, your help will pay off and things will work out well.

Wife

Contentment. To dream of your wife shows contentment in the relationship. However, if you dream of a wife when you are not married, it means that you are about to fall out with your partner, particularly if the relationship is fairly new.

People

We may dream about our family, but equally we will dream of all kinds of people with whom we cross paths in daily life but with whom we have more superficial relationships. We will also dream of fictitious relationships with a range of interesting characters.

General Characters

Boy

Positive image. A boy in a dream, regardless of what sex you are, is a positive image and represents a force that can help you along your path. It sometimes represents a wish for a child, but more often than not stands for activity and action.

Girl

Prospects. If a man dreams of a girl, then this dream could signify romantic encounters. However, regardless of your sex, this dream brings new prospects and news. A man dreaming of being a girl can mean that he is a bit confused about his sexuality.

Man

Masculine drive. A man in a dream brings activity and action; however, the actual meaning of the dream will depend on the situation: what the man is doing, what he is wearing and the colour of his hair. For a woman, the man in the dream can represent a sexual ideal but generally represents activity and masculine drive.

Woman

Change of view. Women in dreams bring changes of viewpoints, but these are not always for the better; they often represent emotional changes. A pregnant woman signifies growth, but in general a woman in a dream indicates that you should use instinct and intuition.

Friends

Friendships in a dream reflect real-life friendships and indicate a happy and active social time to come. New friends in dreams often represent a new circle of friends rather than a particular person and might symbolize a new interest that will be taken up or a club that you will join.

Symbols and Caricatures

Adam and Eve

A strong omen. If Adam and Eve play a part in your dream, it is regarded as a good omen, indicating a new start and that your confidence levels are strengthened by your own truthful recognition of yourself.

Virginity

New beginnings. If you are not a virgin and you dream of virginity, then this can reflect a wish to start something over again. Virginity also represents new projects and so this dream can indicate that you are planning to start a new career just as much as the start of a new relationship.

Crowd

Energy. A crowd – providing it is not unruly – brings energy and hope in a dream. It supports you and allows you to take friends to task. It indicates new outdoor opportunities for you.

Royalty

Happiness and pleasure. Dreaming of royalty – either of meeting them or of actually holding a royal title yourself – indicates a move to escape the monotony of daily life and so it can represent an ideal. In general, dreaming of royalty suggests that some promotional opportunities may be heading your way; however, if the dream does not go well, then this means that you have disclosed an indiscretion and this is about to come back and haunt you. Wearing or being given a crown indicates important offers which will be made and bodes well for the future. Dreaming that you are a prince or princess encapsulates a desire to escape the reality of your current situation.

Politics or Politician

Success and status. Dreaming of politics is an indication of future success; however, if you are dreaming of talking politics with a member of the opposite sex, then it indicates that you will not fulfil your hopes in matters of the heart. Dreaming of running for a political post or working as part of a political campaign indicates that you will achieve success and status, but may also lose out on friendships as a result.

Prostitute

Help at hand. If your dream involves a prostitute, it often means that you will receive help from an unlikely source in solving a problematic issue. If the prostitute is sympathetic, then you are likely to gain the support of others. If she is hardened and brazen in her attitude, then it means you should stay clear of unscrupulous behaviour. If you dream that you are a prostitute, it signifies the outward expression of your sexuality.

Gypsy

Unsettled. If a gypsy appears in your dream, it means that you feel unsettled about something. This dream might indicate a move and certainly you feel restless. A dream such as this is generally good luck, although you may experience some difficulties to start with.

Pirate

Adventure. Dreaming of pirates is an indication that you are seeking emotional excitement.

The sea represents your emotions and pirates seem to add a sense of excitement. The dream could simply mean that you are about to embark on an adventurous business manoeuvre. There is, however, need for caution because just as pirates are untrustworthy, so too can be business colleagues.

Jester

Originality. A court jester was the only person who could make fun of royalty without repercussions. In a dream, the jester means that you can turn your ideas on their head and start in a new direction, with or without your past. You have the ability to see things afresh, and have innovative ideas.

Dwarf

Magical changes. A dwarf is generally lucky in a dream, as it means that the problems that you thought you had are not as large as they seemed and therefore will disappear. The only proviso here is if the dwarf is ugly, as this represents a false friend and distressing problems that could occur.

Love and Marriage

Hugging

Reassurance. If you hug someone in your dream, you are looking for reassurance and their support. If it is a gentle hug, you are simply asking them for support; a stronger hug indicates that significant changes are in store for you. If you are hugging a stranger, though, these changes may not be what you expect.

Kissing

The meaning of this dream lies in the kiss, and the type of kiss will determine the outcome. A gentle affectionate kiss to a loved one is just an expression of affection; however, if the kiss is nonchalant and given with no meaning, then it indicates that you have a false friend.

Love

Happiness. To dream of falling in love reflects a desire for happiness and affection if you are single. If you have a partner, this dream reflects an increased bond between you. If you see other people making love, then this indicates that your life will go well.

Valentine

Romantic problems. If you dream of receiving a valentine, it suggests that you are experiencing problems in your relationship. If you are sending a card in your dream, it indicates that you are not taking advantage of the opportunities that surround you.

Elopement

Disappointment. If you dream that you have eloped with your partner, then it signifies that your relationship will not stand the test of time. Likewise, to dream of encouraging another couple to elope will result in bitter recriminations.

Engagement and Ring

The meaning of an engagement or an engagement ring in a dream depends on who the subject is. If it is your own engagement, it can be that be a warning that you are too idealistic and that an engagement will not sort your relationship out. Conversely if you dream of a friend's engagement, then this often points to good news about an engagement in the future. However, if you dream of your son or daughter getting engaged then it can mean that you fear the loss of your children from your home and to someone else.

If you dream of actually giving or receiving a ring, this is of particular significance, as it indicates a forthcoming marriage or engagement. Rings do not have an end or a beginning, so stand for eternity. To see two rings intertwined in a dream indicates the start of a very close and long-lasting relationship. To dream of broken rings is a signal of a broken relationship and broken hearts.

Jilted

Fear and anxiety. If you dream of being jilted at the altar – or elsewhere – then it suggests you have a fear that your partner will leave you. Despite this, such a dream often means that the relationship is strong and your fears unfounded.

Wedding Celebration

Dreaming of a wedding celebration, particularly of someone else, means that's you are about to hear news of a celebration, wedding or babies. If you are single then it is a good sign that someone will come into your life. However, if it is your own wedding and is in the future, then you need to make sure that your relationship has a sound footing.

Bride

Luck. Dreaming of being or seeing a bride is an indication of luck and celebrations, particularly if it is someone else that is the bride. If it is you, then you need to look at your relationship carefully. If she is your daughter, it is a dream of hope and wishes, but also fear that children are leaving the nest. Be aware, though, that you should take other factors into consideration. For example, if the bride looks unhappy, then there is concern about the relationship.

Groom

Legal notices. To dream of a groom, but not in a wedding situation, indicates indicates that there will be some legal issues to be sorted out in connection with the family before any new venture or marriage can go ahead.

Marriage

Again the context of the dream is important: a dream about someone else's marriage is good news, but if it is your own it can indicated relationship issues, that your relationship is not going as well as it might. This is a warning for you to rethink whether it is really marriage you want. Dreaming of marriage at the start of a relationship suggests that the relationship will not survive.

Adultery

Setbacks. If you dream of committing adultery, it often means you have some secrets that you should keep carefully; trusting someone with these secrets will result in them becoming common knowledge. If you have the same dream on a regular basis, it suggests there is something wrong with the relationship you are in at the moment; you need to sort this out before the relationship breaks down further. Dreaming of adultery can also herald a difficult time in a relationship, where there may be some miscommunication.

Divorce

If you are single or have just embarked upon a relationship, dreaming of divorce indicates that you are not ready for a relationship and it will break up before it has even got off the ground. If you are married, it suggests that the marriage is stable and you have nothing to fear.

beyond earth

Space

Dreaming of the stars brings success in life, while simply being in space suggests a need for isolation. You should be warned, however, not to cut yourself off from others too much. Dreaming of space simply indicates a time of your life when you could do with some time to reflect on your own.

Heavenly Bodies

Planets

An indication of feelings. The planets in dreams have an archetypal astrological imagery and influence specific areas of life and the way in which you approach situations and problems. The planet you see in your dream indicates the area of your life that is affected.

- Mercury represents travel and is an indicator of news and communications
- Venus is the planet of love and brings relationships into focus
- Mars can herald arguments as well as action and activity
- Jupiter in a dream indicates promotion and status
- Saturn is an indication of time and age
- Uranus indicates computers and ideas
- Neptune indicates the mystical side of life
- Pluto is a look at the restrictions we place upon ourselves

Sun

Success. The sun in a dream represents success. If you see the sun rising in a dream, it means you are at the beginning of a period of success. A sunset indicates success looming after a long stretch of hard work and effort. If the sun is high in the midday sky, then your lofty ambitions will succeed.

Moon

Emotions. The moon in a dream represents your emotions and your responses to certain situations. A moon shrouded in mist or clouds represents a relationship which you cannot get through to on an emotional level.

Which phase the Moon is in is also considered significant. If the moon is waxing (going from New Moon to Full Moon), this indicates success in starting new projects and relationships. If the moon is waning (decreasing from Full Moon to New Moon), then it represents the ending of relationships or the solution of problems.

A bright Full Moon indicates success and happiness in relationships. A bright moonlit night also heightens sexual sensitivity and indicates happiness and contentment in a relationship. The effect of everything is increased if you see the moon's reflection in water.

If you dream that you are on the moon, this indicates that you may be being unrealistic about a relationship, reading more into it than actually exists.

Stars

Success. Stars in a dream bring success; if you see just one star, this indicates that success will come in the form of the companionship and influence of a prospective partner. A multitude of stars in your dream indicates success through the help of others, and also means that you will be admired by others. For those with aspirations of stardom, this dream could also herald a burst of activity that might end with the realization of your goals; prepare to work to your full potential.

Comet or Meteor

Sudden changes or inspiration. Seeing a comet or meteor, or finding a meteorite, in your dream heralds rapid changes for you. These could be unexpected and quite profound; they might be emotional breakthroughs concerning a new viewpoint in relationships, or in work you will find new ideas – and if you are a bit of a boffin, a new discovery awaits you. Your life is about to undergo a boon of sudden changes – so be prepared to make the most of opportunities that will present themselves. This effect will not last long – generally a day – so seize the chance before it disappears.

Space Connections

Eclipse

Worry. If you dream of an eclipse, it can indicate that you are feeling unsure of yourself. An eclipse of the moon is believed to refer to health issues which may need to be checked

out. A solar eclipse tends to bring business problems that need to be sorted.

Time

Time for action. If you dream about time in a very obvious or significant way – looking at a watch, for example – then this is your subconscious telling you to get on with things straightaway rather than putting them off. The dream is telling you to stop simply waiting for things to happen and activate your plans now.

Rocket

Romantic liaisons. Rockets in a dream indicate sexual matters. A rocket at take-off indicates a happy time in a relationship; a rocket returning to Earth may mean that your relationship is coming down to Earth with a bump.

Religion

Religion is a very emotive subject to many and can therefore have a potent effect – dreaming of being in hell, for example, represents a warning to stop acting against your true beliefs. If you dream of religion in general, then it indicates that you are content with your own spirituality, particularly if outside (in contrast to dreaming of being inside a church, which may indicate less comfort with your spiritual identity.)

Religious Imagery

Religious Icons

Religious upbringing will influence the religious characters and icons that you see in a dream, with the imagery tailored to your religious background. Whatever your beliefs, though, religious icons in dreams seem to have a powerful influence on the dreamer.

 Angels: Seen as a positive omen, and indicate that your wishes will be granted. Cherubs also hint at forthcoming happiness.

 The Devil: Symbolizes your 'inner devils' and indicates the need to take responsibility for your own actions in order for you to experience freedom. It often indicates a situation where the dreamer feels tied down, but where it is up to the dreamer to find their own solution instead of blaming others.

God: The appearance of God in your dreams indicates contentment with your situation.

 Rabbi: To dream of a rabbi is a powerful omen, whatever your religion, and symbolizes a friend who will make an effort to understand your problems.

 Priest: If you see the local priest in your dreams, then you are probably ill at ease with a recent event, whereas to dream of a bishop or archbishop suggests that you need to ask someone for advice, but do not know how to go about it.

Prayer

Contemplation. If you dream that you are in prayer, then it means that you need to reflect on what is happening around you. If you hear others pray, then it indicates that you will get the support of others.

Hymn

Good news. If you hear hymns in your dreams, it represents good news coming to you from someone older, and this will lead to a rise in your status amongst the people around you. It is also an indication that you will be put in a position of responsibility and authority.

Mass

Support of others. To dream that you are at a church Mass indicates that at the moment you feel alone and could do with the support of others. An outside Mass means that eventually you will gain the support you desire, but if you are inside a church, it indicates that this assistance will not be forthcoming and you will have to cope alone.

Bible

Rewards and help from others. If you dream of the Bible, then it indicates that you will receive kindness in return for compassion you have recently shown towards others. The psalm that is seen in the dream can give an indication of the identity of the person who will show you this kindness.

Commandments

Rules and regulations. To dream about the Ten Commandments indicates that you have not been true to yourself or to others and that some people will feel let down by your attitude. The Commandment you have broken in the dream will give an indication of the lesson you need to address.

Christmas

Family celebrations. To dream of Christmas implies that you are looking forward to celebrations and family reunions. It indicates social gatherings in the near future and domestic happiness.

Resurrection

Preparation. Dreaming of the Resurrection suggests that, although you are confused by events around you at the moment, you will find that they are soon sorted out.

Heaven or Paradise

Change. To dream of heaven or paradise indicates that you are preparing for changes in your life; these may not be easy to cope with, but you will have to embrace them if you are going to be able to relax and enjoy the future.

Hell

Fear. If you dream of being in hell, it indicates that you may be acting against your true beliefs in a particular circumstance, and the dream is a warning against acting purely for financial gain, hinting that your behaviour may cause you to lose friends.

Judgement

Understanding. If you dream of the Day of Judgement or if you play out the judgement in a court of law in your dream, it is an indication that you are about to gain an understanding of your need to change your viewpoints in order to progress.

Sacred Places

Church

To see a church from the outside in a dream is a positive sign; to be inside a church can be interpreted as a bad omen. Outside a church indicates celebrations on the way. Being inside a church in your dream suggests that you are in a difficult situation with another person.

Altar

News. To dream of standing at an altar signifies some unexpected news and a celebration. This might mean that a marriage is about to be announced or occur, or it could simply bring some welcome changes to your life.

Convent

Reflection and solitude. To dream that you are in a convent represents a wish to have some time to yourself for thought and reflection. It is an indication that perhaps events have been too hectic recently and you feel tired and drained.

Vatican

Influential meetings. If you dream of being at the Vatican, it suggests that you will meet someone who will be able to influence your career progression. However, you will need to show them respect first, as they can be quite demanding.

Synagogue

Social status. If you climb to the top, then it means that you will achieve status in the eyes of others. If you are inside the synagogue, however, this suggests you are experiencing difficulties with other people that need to be resolved.

Fantasy and the Supernatural

Magical and fantastical motifs have much capacity for representing feelings, people and events in alternative ways to shed new light – a single witch, for example, can represent a wise and trusted friend.

Magic and the Occult

Witch

Celebrations. Witches in your dream suggest that there will soon be a party, and friends to mingle with. A single witch may also represent a wise and trusted friend who will be able to help you deal with a particular problem you are facing.

Wizard

Help at hand. If you dream of a wizard, then it indicates that help is at hand from an unknown source. Remember, though, that you will need to show some perseverance if the problem is to be solved. If the wizard seems to be working against your interests in the dream, this suggests that you know someone who is behaving in a way that has a detrimental effect on you.

Dragon

Energy. Dragons in dreams are a potent symbol of what lies ahead. They often indicate help in career choices and situations, as they can give rewards for effort. A dragon can also represent an influential person who will be instrumental in your success.

Phantom or Spirit

Message. Seeing a phantom in your dreams may mean that someone is trying to communicate a message to you. Generally, this is a message of good news that you should take on board but you will have to try to work out what the message is to understand this dream fully. As you can be more psychically in tune when you are asleep, it is possible that you have managed to communicate with a spirit of some sort. If the phantom is frightening, then it is an indication that you need to act sooner rather than later.

Aliens

New acquaintances. If you dream of an alien encounter, it means that you are about to meet someone new who will have a strong influence in your life and will bring about a change of direction for you. If you were the alien in your dream, this suggests that part of your personality is trying to emerge which could surprise or shock you and those around you.

Fairies

Granted wishes. To see a fairy in a dream means that you are about to be successful in something that you have planned. You will find that others are favourable to your ideas and will help you out as much as possible.

Giants

Listen carefully. If a giant appears in a dream, it means that you are about to hear or be told something to which you should pay great attention. The giant, of course, signifies a matter of great size and import and the news will have a significant effect on your life.

Unicorn

True romantic prospects. The appearance of a unicorn in a dream is a good omen, symbolizing new prospects for true romance entering your life. A unicorn is often dreamt of at the start of a very significant and long-term relationship and indicates your happiness with the situation.

Vampire

Conflict with others. If you dream of meeting a vampire, it is a warning that there could be an individual who is becoming an emotional drain on you – perhaps revealed in who the vampire resembles. To dream that you are a vampire indicates a wish to have control of others and can also be read as a warning that you may be abusing a position of trust.

Powers and Places

Invisibility

Change. Dreaming you are invisible means that changes are about to occur over which you will have no control. If you dream that you are invisible in someone else's house, then this may indicate that you are psychically picking up on a particular experience they are having or situation they are in.

Metamorphosis

Change. If you dream that you can metamorphose into something, you should pay attention to the creature you find yourself able to change into: this will indicate the abilities that you need to cultivate. You need to adapt and change certain aspects of your character to be able to move forward in your life. Correlate the meaning of this dream with the creature featured in your dream for a full interpretation.

Labyrinth

Emotional decisions. The labyrinth in a dream is an indication that you are facing obstacles in your emotional life. Decisions need to be made and the ease with which you find the way out of your dream labyrinth will dictate how easily you will be able to overcome those obstacles on waking. To get to the centre of the labyrinth bodes well for self-discovery and aspects relating to self-actualization.

Clairvoyant

To dream of seeing a clairvoyant indicates that you need help with planning your future. There are a lot of options open to you at the moment and you need to give everything proper consideration. Occupational changes are due soon and you need to have a clear idea of what lies ahead down the different paths you could choose. If you happen to be a clairvoyant, this dream is a confirmation of your attributes and abilities.

Astrology and Horoscopes

To dream of having your horoscope read or your astrological birth chart drawn up suggests that you need to sit down and plan your future. Important changes will shortly take place and you need to work out how to make the best of the opportunities that present themselves. If you take this advice on board, you will achieve success in all that you do.

food and environment

Vegetation

To dream of a garden indicates pleasure, while a forest has much more ambiguous properties. Lilies can anticipate happiness, but beware if they are wilting... Trees, plants and flowers all have a significance in our dreams.

Trees and Plants

Forest

Obstacles and opportunities. The meaning of the forest will depend very much on the situation. If you are alone in the forest, then someone will let you down. Hiding or being lost in a forest indicates obstacles that you must accept and face to be able to proceed; you may have to undertake a long journey to resolve the issue. On the other hand, if you feel that you are enjoying the forest walk, then it can indicate that you will gain status and fame.

Tree

Lucky in love but not in work. To dream of planting and growing trees is an indication of a new love in your life and relationships will go well. However, to dream of climbing trees indicates that finances will be severely tested as the amount of effort you are putting into work at the moment does not seem to give a particularly good return.

Root

Reward for effort. Success is presaged if dreaming of roots of any kind. The indications are that you have put in a lot of work recently and that, with your continued hard work, you will get the success that you deserve. Roots that appear above ground are drawing your attention to being more assertive in your deliberations or a rival will aggressively take your opportunity.

Palm

Holidays. To see a palm tree in your dreams is an indication that you should consider booking that holiday. You have been overdoing it recently and you feel you need to relax, so now is a good time to plan holiday arrangements. You can also expect at this time news from someone abroad.

Weeds

Undesirable friends. If you dream of weeds, then it indicates people around you who are having a bad effect on you and your plans. If you dream that you are weeding the garden, then you will succeed in getting rid of their influence on you.

Mistletoe

Fertility. Dreaming of mistletoe for someone young is a symbol of sexual desires and fertility. It is therefore a dream of positive news to someone in a relationship. In business matters, this dream heralds a need for greater patience.

Hedge

Meeting other people. A hedge represents an obstacle and therefore to jump through or walk through a hedge indicates that you will succeed in your undertakings, which will involve others. For someone to walk through the gap in a hedge indicates a new friend who will break down the barriers that you often put up.

Ivy

Friendship. If you dream of ivy, whether growing indoors or out, it indicates that there are a lot of people around you who are willing to help you sort out problems, whatever the issue – you only need to ask and the help will be there.

Bramble

Obstacles. Brambles as a dream omen represent obstacles that you have to fight your way through. If you get through them, then you will be successful but you need to show a lot of perseverance and effort. To be pricked by the thorns means that you have some legal issues to deal with as well. If you escape without infection in your dream, you will survive the problems raised.

Flowers

Flower

Good fortune. To see flowers in your dream generally brings the promise of good fortune and especially romance. Flowers wilting indicate a relationship dying. In business dealings, it is a warning not to be overconfident. Artificial flowers mean that you could be acting against your own beliefs and you need to think carefully about your motives, unless, of course, you suffer from hay fever, when this dream indicates that maybe you are being overly cautious in a situation.

Marigold

Contentment. If you dream of marigolds, it shows that you will be content in life, even though you will not have much money. It seems that you will also be happy, as financial issues are not important to you.

Primrose

Passion. If you dream of a primrose, then it indicates a very hot and steamy relationship. It is also a very hot-headed one and there will be plenty of arguments, and it is unlikely to stand the test of time.

Violet

New affection. If you dream of violets, then there is someone nearby who has not shown an interest in you up to now, but whose affections begin to awaken. You could find they start to make approaches to you over the course of the next few weeks.

Lily

Happiness is presaged if you see or are given lilies in a dream. If the lilies are wilting or poorly presented, then the signs are that a relationship is about to enter a difficult phase, involving stubbornness and a lack of compromise by both parties.

Rose

Romance. This is the ultimate flower of love and, if it appears in your dreams, you can certainly take it as a sign that love will soon blossom. The relationship is shown to be one of dedication and love, leading to confidence and happiness.

Daisy

If you dream of daisies out in the fields, then this indicates a happy time, but if they are in a vase indoors or in a bunch, then it signifies a sadness connected to a relationship that is not going according to plan.

Poppy

Remembrance. So ingrained on the subconscious are the memories of the two World Wars that now the red poppy in a dream is a sign of remembrance. It hints that you will remember someone who has departed.

Food

Food is a recurring theme in dreams. If you are hungry in your dream, it may be that you are unhappy with the way things are going in your life. Dreaming of shopping suggests success in your endeavours. The multitude of different food items you may see or taste can suggest all manner of portents.

Vegetables and Grain

Vegetable

To dream that you are eating a variety of vegetables hints that, although you seem to have hit the jackpot with a project, the passage of time will reveal that you have actually been exploited for your talents. To grow a variety of vegetables in a dream signifies that your possessiveness in a relationship may lead to its demise.

Bean

Worries and illness. Growing beans hints that there will be sickness for youngsters around you. Eating them foretells that a close loved one will suffer a bout of illness. Beans on toast implies that you will lose valuable friendships through lack of consideration and not helping in their hour of need.

Lettuce

Jealousy. You will have to watch out if you dream of eating lettuce, as you are showing signs of being jealous of someone else's position; if you are not careful, you will end up in an embarrassing situation of your own making. To see lettuce growing suggests that you may gain a longed-for prize that has been in your sights for some time.

Cabbage

Calamity. Dreaming of eating or cooking cabbages is an indicator of all sorts of problems about to descend on you. Relationship issues and financial problems are highlighted by this dream and they will be difficult to resolve, possibly even leading to total collapse.

Tomato

Fertility and love. Tomatoes in a dream represent love and fertility. In a dream, this could be informing you that a relationship is about to start. For a woman in particular, it means that you could be thinking of having children and you are in a very fertile period of your life.

Onions

Onions represent envy from others towards you. If you see them growing, it can mean you may have to tactfully ward off the opposition without arousing their envy. To eat onions in your dream implies that sparks will fly and tension will surround you.

Garlic

Protection. Garlic has long been associated with protection from vampires and, in a dream, garlic indicates that you have protection from people doing you some harm. If you dream of eating garlic with a partner, it suggests that you are more interested in financial stability than love.

Potato

Good luck all round. If you dream of potatoes, it indicates that not only will you enter a state of happiness in your home but also that work will see improvements and your income will also be significantly better.

Carrot

Financial luck. Dreaming of carrots means that your income is going to increase shortly, through extending your relations. If you are a single woman, then it may suggest that your future husband is about to enter your life and together you will have a large family.

Mushroom

Financial rewards. Dreaming of eating mushrooms indicates that your finances are due to 'mushroom' soon and that you will be able to cash in on your investments. You have worked hard but you will now be able to sit back and relax a little. To see wild mushrooms suggests that you may well be searching for a freer lifestyle.

Fruit

Strawberry

Happy in love. If you dream that you are eating strawberries, it indicates that you are content with the relationship you are in; this is a particularly good omen for a relationship that has just started, suggesting a strong long-term future.

Blackberry

Illness and financial bad luck. Blackberries in dreams are not good news, as they symbolize loss. Finances could be in trouble and you may need to reorganize them carefully in order to prevent any losses. Eating blackberries is a sign you could be ill – or about to fall ill if the blackberries are unripe.

Plum

Career enhancement. If you dream of eating plums, like the nursery rhyme of Jack Horner who pulled out a plum which turned out to be title deeds, plums in dreams represent property gains connected with land investments. If they are dried or tinned, however, this indicates that your collateral and finances are bound up with property problems.

Apple

Temptation. Apples are considered a good omen, particularly if you are eating one in your dream. It can also be a sign of new love and, if you are not sure yet, then you may be led into temptation earlier in the relationship than perhaps you had planned. Apples are considered to be magical in a dream because, if you chop them in half, you can see the five pointed stars or pentagrams used by witches and believed to have magical properties.

Banana

A relationship based only on sexual attraction. To dream of a banana indicates that you are about to enter a relationship where there is strong initial sexual attraction but little else. This is also a forewarning that the relationship is unlikely to stand the test of time.

Orange

Choice of lovers. If you dream of eating oranges, then it indicates that you are in a situation where you may have to choose between a number of admirers who are after your affection. At the moment you are undecided but you will be forced to choose between them in the near future.

Lemon

Financial issues. Lemons in a dream can suggest you need to be aware of finances. It is time to tighten your belt and take a more economical approach to your household budget. If you dream of sucking on a lemon, then you need to be careful that you do not cause an embarrassment to yourself or to others because of your limited finances.

Peach

Pleasure – but at a risk. Dreaming of peaches indicates that you will have to take a risk in the near future but the end result will be worth it – you just need to persevere.

Grape

Joy. Dreaming of grapes is an indication of joy and hints that a celebration party will go extremely well. White (green) grapes are considered better than black in terms of the intensity of the celebration and its significance. There is, however, a hidden warning in such dreams against overindulgence – suggesting that success can go to your head and that you may become intoxicated with a sense of self-importance.

Pineapple

Social happiness. Eating a pineapple indicates a social success and that you will find yourself in an elevated position. You will also be able to go on an exotic holiday with family or friends as you take advantage of this success.

Nuts

Walnut

Obstacle in love. Dreaming of a walnut indicates there is a communication issue in a relationship. If you are able to crack the walnut in your dream, then it indicates that you will be able to resolve the problem. If you are unable to crack the walnut, then your partner is likely to meet someone else.

Almond

Temporary domestic issues. Almonds in a dream bring sorrow and this dream is about teaching you to snap out of feeling disillusioned. There will be some temporary setbacks for your family, but they are only fleeting and you will be able to move forward again shortly.

Chestnut

To dream of chestnuts indicates that there can be some temporary delays to your plans, but they will not cause a problem in the long run. The significance of this dream is that you must ignore delays for they will be temporary and the more you press ahead, the greater your success.

Herbs and Spices

Parsley

Rewards for effort. If you dream of eating or growing parsley, it shows that, although you will have to undertake hard work, you will be rewarded for your efforts in the long run. Family issues are also heightened and you may decide to add to the family.

Sage

Change of financial circumstances. To dream of sage indicates that you may have to be careful with your finances over the coming months. This does not need to be anything drastic, but extravagance should be put on hold for a while. This is also a time for being cautious with investments and it may be better to put some decisions off for a while.

Mint

Health improvements. Dreaming of mint is quite common and it is possible that it is related to residue from toothpaste. It is also thought that mint in a dream signifies a feeling of refreshment; if you have been tired or ill recently, you will find your health improves, giving you a sense of refreshing buoyancy, particularly in matters involving communications.

Pepper

Watch your reactions. To dream of pepper indicates that you need to watch for being hot-headed. Arguments are too easy for you to get involved in. If you dream of your tongue being affected by pepper, then it is a warning not to react to gossip.

Nutmeg

Avoid being used. If you dream of cooking with nutmeg or even eating it, then it indicates a social party to take place soon at which someone will make a romantic play for you. He or she is not the one for you, however, and you should take the dream as a warning to steer well clear.

Meat

Meat

Financial achievements. If the meat is raw, it signifies that you will not fulfil your life's ambitions. If you dream of cooking meat or cooked meat on a plate, then you will accomplish a lot in life; changes in the near future will help you on your way financially and you will do well.

Poultry

Extravagance. To dream that you are eating or cooking poultry indicates that you will have to be careful in dealing with domestic financial issues. This dream is a hint that you are inclined to overspend – a fault you should watch carefully in the near future.

Beef

Tragedy. If the beef in your dream has gone off, it indicates physical harm to the body. To witness either eating or cooking rotten beef means that there is likely to be much suffering followed by a period of instability. To see quality beef cooked and served is a harbinger of joy in business and love situations.

Pork

Property achievements. If you dream of pork, it suggests that you will do well in property dealings. If you are eating pork in your dream, then it is a warning to be careful in these property transactions. To serve pork indicates that you will be involved in heavy negotiations before achieving your goals.

Cooking

Baking

Domestic happiness. To dream of baking indicates that you are satisfied with your domestic situation. It can also signify that there is going to be a big family reunion and a happy celebration for you to plan.

Roasting

Arguments over indiscretion. To dream that you are roasting a piece of meat suggests that an argument may break out and you are likely to give your partner a hard time over something that he or she has done, particularly in matters involving a love triangle.

Frying

Problems in love. If you dream that you are frying, then it indicates that there are issues in a relationship that need to be resolved before they become too intense. There may also be another possible relationship on the horizon, but you must be careful here not to jump from the frying pan into the fire.

Boiling

Self-control. If you dream of boiling water or other liquid, then it indicates that you are in danger of losing your temper and self-control over an issue at the moment. You need to try to keep calm over the situation and the problem will dissipate.

Savoury Food

Bread

Family state. If the bread is fresh – and particularly if you have dreamt of baking the bread yourself – then this indicates contentment in the family. However, if the bread is stale, then there is a problem in the family and perhaps the feeling is that the relationship has gone stale and may require some changes to improve circumstances.

Butter

Good health. Butter in a dream represents health and energy as well as being an indication that you will succeed in small projects. This dream can herald some small financial benefits.

Milk

Good health. To dream of milk is a general dream indicating good health; the more milk you see, the better your health and joy will be. Goat's milk is meant to be good for financial business. If you dream of milking animals, then this is even better for financial success, though if the cow is restless it may take a little longer than anticipated.

Cream

Good fortune. Regardless of your occupation, dreaming of cream indicates that business is about to enter a prosperous period. It is especially good for businesses involving share-dealing or the stock market – you will do exceptionally well.

Cheese

A warning. It is said that eating cheese before you retire to bed will give you nightmares. Cheese in a dream will have its meaning modified by the type of cheese you see. Gorgonzola and other strong-smelling cheeses can herald career problems, while Cheddar and Edam relate to love. Dreaming of grating cheese suggests that you have to sort out one or two financial issues.

Rice

Family gain. Dreaming of cooking rice indicates fertility and children, and that there will be a family celebration for a new arrival soon. More generally, to see grains of rice in your dream is a good sign, symbolizing success, prosperity, luck, fertility and warm friendships.

Soup

Good effort after bad. To hear the slurping of soup in a dream portends new and exciting liaisons through party invites. To drink cold soup suggests that a love life issue is leading to the realization that a companion is not going to listen to your needs – cut your losses and let the relationship go. To dream of drinking hot soup means that you will have to fight on with a project of worth, if you are to come out the other end with a successful resolution.

Sweet Food

Sweets

If you dream about giving or eating sweets, then this indicates a happy time. The only exception to this is if you dream of eating sticky toffee, which hints that you need to be careful not to repeat gossip, otherwise you could find yourself falling out with some friends.

Cake

A joyous time. Cakes indicate happy times, although the type of cake will reveal more about this time. If you see a wedding cake, then this can obviously suggest a wedding is in the air. A thickly iced cake denotes a party; it could be a birthday or the news of the birth of a child. Cream cakes indicate promotion and celebration at work, while a plain sponge cake can indicate a family gathering.

Biscuits

Disputes. If you dream of eating biscuits, then petty arguments could break out in your family. These are shown to be easily resolved if you can get the family to sit down and work things out.

Chocolate

Pleasure seeker. Regardless of whether you dream of eating chocolate or drinking chocolate, it is an indication that you are trying to seek pleasure: this could suggest that relationships are not going well and that you are in the mood for finding someone new to light up your life.

Jam

Appreciations. Jam on the table indicates contentment with a family situation. Friends and family will also appreciate the amount of work that you have done for them lately and will be keen to help you out of any difficulties that you are now facing.

Jelly

Social pleasure. To dream of making jelly indicates a get-together soon of family and children. However, to dream that you are eating jelly indicates that you feel all your time is being taken up with unimportant things.

Ice Cream

Business success. If you dream of eating ice cream, it suggests some small business successes shortly. Ice cream can also mean that family life is good; however, to see melted or spilt ice cream indicates that there could be some family tensions in the air.

Drink

Drinking cool water is considered a good omen, particularly if you are due to face exams, as it symbolizes refreshing the mind. Drinking fizzy drinks such as cola indicates that events in your life will be moving fast. Certain drinks are said to indicate romantic liaisons, but if you are drinking from the bottle in your dreams, this is unromantic and you will lose out in the relationship.

Alcohol

Spirits

Warning. If in your dream you are drinking spirits and you keep to safe limits, then it indicates a celebration. If you drink to excess, however, it indicates that you will find yourself in an embarrassing situation and may let others down.

Wine

Celebration. If you dream of drinking wine, then it indicates a celebration in the near future. If you are a young person dreaming of drinking wine, it means you are shortly to have a relationship with a wealthy person.

Cocktails

Immoral life. If you dream of cocktails, then it indicates that you have been giving an impression to some that you are home-loving or, if single, a serious student, when in reality you have been spending every night at clubs and pubs.

Whisky

Meanness. If you dream of whisky, then it indicates that you will lose friendships by being mean and miserly, and that others regard you as being only interested in yourself.

Cider

Good luck in exams. Dreams of cider bring good luck, particularly if you are a student and are to undertake exams shortly. On the negative side, though, you will need to keep yourself from being involved in some gossip.

Beer

Good fortune. If the beer in your dream was tasty and had a good head, then it indicates good news in business dealings. However, if the beer was flat, then not only is this a sign of a dubious landlord, but also you are warned not to trust your friends, as they are about to let you down.

Hot Drinks

Cocoa

Pleasure seeker. If you dream of drinking hot cocoa or chocolate, it is an indication that you are seeking new sexual pleasures; it may be that your relationship is not going well, and this dream means that you are in the mood for finding someone new to light up your life.

Tea

Popularity. If you dream of drinking tea, then it indicates that you will do well socially over the next few weeks. However, to dream simply of the teapot brewing, with no drinking, indicates that you will be apologetic over a liaison that has caused upset to someone else.

Coffee

News. If you dream of drinking coffee, then it indicates that you are shortly to receive some important news, which you should act upon as soon as possible. If you spill coffee, though, take it as a warning not to act on the news you receive.

Weather and Nature

The natural atmosphere of your dream is always important. What is the weather like? What season is it? The seasons in particular represent time frames. So, if it is autumn and you dream of spring, it suggests that the issues about which you dreamt are likely to take six months to resolve. To dream of winter when it is not winter indicates that financial issues will be resolved by then. Autumn brings new friendships, spring new relationships and the summer brings news.

Weather Conditions

Heat and Cold

An indication of feelings. Hot weather in your dreams is considered a good omen, as it brings with it success and opportunities. Cold weather means that you feel depressed about a situation and in a dream represents the need for hard work. Wet weather brings emotional problems that need to be resolved before you can move forward.

Rain

Money issues. Rain in dreams relates to your financial circumstances. A light pouring of rain suggests that you will have one or two minor financial issues to sort out, but if the rain is heavier, this anticipates that you will be able to spend some of the money you have saved for a rainy day. To hear raindrops on the roof indicates that you will be secure in your home – just as long as the roof is not leaking. To be drenched by rain means that you are about to receive a substantial sum of money. A thunderstorm or monsoon represents a business venture that is about to take off and, although you will be working harder, you will be rewarded for the effort.

Rainbow

A dream comes true. If you dream of a rainbow, then it indicates that you will find happiness and reward soon. Rainbows signify promotions and success. If your dream included your partner, it indicates the fulfilment of your desires and hopes from the relationship, and suggests that your commitments are about to bear fruit.

Clouds

Approaching conditions. Clouds in dreams represent the conditions that you face over the next few weeks. If the clouds are white and the sky is bright, then you can expect positive results, particularly with romance. If clouds are obscuring the sun, then it indicates obstacles to overcome. Storm clouds suggest that there will be problems to face, but that if you persevere, you will succeed in your endeavours.

Storm

Obstacles to overcome. To dream of a storm indicates that you may have some problem facing you but that you will be able to battle through and come out the other side. The intensity of the storm will dictate the level of difficulty you will face in the course of these problems, but the positive side of such dreams is that they show that the problems are surmountable.

Lightning

A bolt from the blue. Dreaming of lightning indicates that you will soon find yourself in the middle of some unexpected events. However, just as everything feels fresher after a thunderstorm, so your dream represents a renewed vigour and a continuation of some old projects, as well as the start of some new ones.

Snow

A positive omen. If you are walking through the snow in your dream, it is an indication of contentment in a relationship and bodes well for the future. If the snow is heavy, you will be rewarded greatly for the efforts that you have put in. If the snow is light, then it is a good time to look at business investments.

Ice

Warning. If you dream of walking or especially slipping on ice, it is considered to be a warning that you need to pay attention to your finances or you could get into trouble. An iceberg indicates that you are facing a hidden obstacle. To see an icicle or ice-covered trees, however, indicates that, given time, your dreams and aspirations will come to fruition.

Fog

Problems. To see fog in your dreams means that there is a problem in your life. If the fog is at sea or seems to be coming off the sea, this indicates that you have an emotional problem to sort out. If it is foggy on land, this indicates problems at work. If the fog clears or you hear a foghorn, then it indicates that the problem will disappear in the course of time.

Wind

Ideas. In a dream, the wind represents learning and ideas. A gentle wind gives good steady progress. However, if the wind is gusty, then it can mean that your ideas keep stalling. If the wind is very strong, then it may be a hard job for you to succeed, especially if you dream that you have been blown over.

Water

Emotional feelings. Water in your dreams is a representation of your emotions and also how you are reacting to relationships at the moment. The calmer the water, the less you feel any emotional problems. Murky or rough water indicates that you have deep emotional issues to deal with.

Sea

Emotional issues. The sea represents emotional issues: the rougher the weather and the choppier the sea, the more problems you face. If you are able to sail through the sea in the course of your dream, then your problems will ease. Crossing the sea also indicates that your opportunities for company will increase through cross-cultural experiences.

Sky

An indication of your state of mind. If the sky is clear, then it indicates you are content or even happy with your current situation. If the sky clears and brightens up in the course of your dream, it suggests that any problems you have will soon disappear. If the sky darkens, then this can indicate a worsening of the situation.

Disasters

Fire

Impending trouble. If you see fire in a dream, it indicates trouble ahead. Problems will pursue you, particularly if you are burnt by the fire in your dream. If you manage to put out the fire, then you will be able to deal with the obstacles you face, even if they appear insurmountable to begin with. A fire also signifies strength and determination and so, if the fire seems to be under control, then it indicates that you have strength of purpose and will be able to deal with the problems that are facing you. Flames in a fire can provide a message of where the trouble will come from and you might be able to see pictures in the flames.

Earthquake

Change. If you live in an area subject to earthquakes, then such a dream can act as a warning to prepare you for minor difficulties. However, if you do not live in an earthquake area, then the indication is far more cataclysmic, as it suggests profound changes in your life and the need for major adjustments. These changes will be brought about by circumstances beyond your control. If your response to the earthquake in the dream is fear, then you will prosper. Neighbourhood losses will reunite the community if you feel the presence of God in this dream.

Volcano

Dangerous situation. If your dream includes a volcano, this is a major warning of situations that could get out of control. If the volcano is extinct or inactive, then it is a warning to delay decisions. A smoking volcano indicates a relationship that is underhand and needs to be looked at carefully. An erupting volcano indicates that disputes and arguments that will be difficult to resolve are about to erupt and may mean drastic changes are made to your life.

Flood

Emotional obstacles. Dreaming of a flood is indicative of emotional issues that need to be sorted out. If the flood is gentle, not above knee height, and quickly recedes, then your problems will be easily solved. If the water is muddy and the flood chest-height, then it indicates the problem will be harder to resolve. If you are swept away in the flood, this suggests that a person is using you for their own selfish emotional needs.

Drought

Difficulties to overcome. To dream of a drought suggests that some difficult times lie ahead, but that the situation can be overcome with some careful preparation. This might mean putting some money aside for added security in the future.

Further Reading

Altman, Jack, *1001 Dreams: An Illustrated Guide to Dreams and Their Meanings*, Duncan Baird Publishers, 2002

Cheung, Theresa, *The Dream Dictionary from A to Z: The Ultimate A-Z to Interpret the Secrets of Your Dreams*, Harper Element, 2009

Crisp, Tony, *Dream Dictionary: An A to Z Guide to Understanding Your Unconscious Mind*, Bantam Doubleday Dell, 2002

Dee, Nerys, *Understand Dreams: What They Are and How to Interpret Them*, Thorsons, 2000

Fontana, David, *The New Secret Language of Dreams: The Illustrated Key to Understanding the Mysteries of the Unconscious*, Duncan Baird Publishers, 2008

Friedman, Joe, *The Dream Workbook: The Practical Guide to Understanding Your Dreams and Making Them Work for You*, Carroll & Brown Ltd, 2007

Hamilton-Parker, Craig, *The Hidden Meaning of Dreams*, Sterling, 2000

MacGregor, Trish and MacGregor, Rob, *The Complete Dream Dictionary: A Bedside Guide to Knowing What Your Dreams Mean*, Adams Media Corporation, 2005

Mallon, Brenda, *The Dream Bible: The Definitive Guide to Every Dream Symbol Under the Moon*, Godsfield Press, 2003

Pierce, Chuck D., *When God Speaks: How to Interpret Dreams, Visions, Signs and Wonders*, Regal Books, 2005

Reading, Mario, *The Watkins Dictionary of Dreams: The Ultimate Resource for Dreamers*, Watkins Publishing, 2007

Robinson, Stearn and Corbett, Tom, *The Dreamer's Dictionary: Understand the Deeper Meanings of Your Dreams*, Thorsons, 1996

Royston, Robin, *The Hidden Power of Dreams: A Guide to Understanding Their Meaning*, Bantam Books, 2007

Scott, Elizabeth, *Your Dreams: What They Really Mean*, Clarion, 2004

Starr, Fiona and Zucker, Johnny, *Dream Themes: A Guide to Understanding Your Dreams*, Barnes and Noble, 2003

Websites

www.analysedreams.co.uk
The Analyse Dreams website, with information on common dreams, themes, types and dream analysis, as well as an 'ask an expert' facility.

www.dream.dictionary-dream.info
This dream dictionary site provides a basic A to Z of symbols and types of dreams, using a search or browse function.

www.dreamforth.com
The DreamForth website is divided into sections on dream interpretation, themes and a dictionary, allowing you to search its online database for all sorts of dream information.

www.dreammoods.com
The website of Dream Moods, which aims to help you make sense of your dreams and, through them, gain a better perspective on your life. It includes a dream dictionary.

www.dreamsymbolism.info
Help with understanding the type of dream you have had and how it might relate to your waking life, with leading questions about recent events that will guide you.

www.easy-dream-interpretation.com
A guide to self-analysis, with tips on how to remember and record your dreams, and information on symbols such as animals, colours and numbers.

www.paranormality.com/dream_dictionary.shtml
An A to Z of the meaning of 10,000 dreams, interpreted by Gustavus Hindman Miller.

www.psychicguild.com/dream
The website of the Universal Psychic Guild, which gives general information about dreams, as well as having an online dream dictionary.

www.sleeps.com
This is the website of Dream Central, with all manner of dreams information, including facts about why and when we dream, a dream dictionary and dream analysis.

www.templeofdreams.com
The Temple of Dreams is an online community centred around psychological healing and spiritual growth. Its website contains basic information about dreams, including lucid dreams.

www.thecuriousdreamer.com
The Curious Dreamer is a free online dream analysis service, allowing you to look up the meaning of your dream on its dream dictionary and analyse it with the help of their articles.

Index